DEMOCRACY MARCHES

DEMOCRACY MARCHES

By
JULIAN HUXLEY

Essay Index Reprint Series

 BOOKS FOR LIBRARIES PRESS
FREEPORT, NEW YORK

Copyright © 1941 by Julian S. Huxley
All rights reserved

Reprinted 1970 by arrangement with
Harper & Row, Publishers, Inc.

INTERNATIONAL STANDARD BOOK NUMBER:
0-8369-1757-X

LIBRARY OF CONGRESS CATALOG CARD NUMBER:
75-117813

PRINTED IN THE UNITED STATES OF AMERICA

Contents

	PAGE
PREFACE *by the Author*	vii
FOREWORD *by Lord Horder, G.C.V.O.*	ix
I. THE UNIFYING EFFECT OF WAR	1
II. THE BRITISH BRAND OF DEMOCRACY	9
III. THE BRITISH SOCIAL SERVICES	20
IV. SOCIAL SERVICE AND DEMOCRACY	30
V. SOCIAL STANDARDS	41
VI. HEALTH IN A DEMOCRATIC BRITAIN	49
VII. THE DEMOCRATIZATION OF EDUCATION	58
VIII. PLANNING AND DEMOCRACY	68
IX. THE DEVELOPMENT OF BACKWARD AREAS	80
X. DEMOCRACY BETWEEN NATIONS	93
XI. DISINTEGRATION AND REINTEGRATION	104
XII. THE NEW DEMOCRATIC SOCIETY	114

Preface

THIS little book had its origin in a series of wireless talks to North America which I gave last winter and spring. I was asked to make my main theme the history of the social services in this country. However, it soon became apparent that it would be necessary to speak of present trends and possible future developments as well as past achievement, and to sketch these in against a background provided by some general analysis of democracy and its trends and transformations.

Democracy Marches was the general title under which my own and a number of other series of talks were given: I make no apologies for having stolen it for this book. Democracy does march—at least, it can be marching. It was very salutary for me to have to clear my own thoughts on the direction which the march of democracy was taking and the method by which its future advance might be achieved. If this little book helps others to think about these vital problems, I shall be well content.

I cannot refer individually to all the friends who have helped me with facts and criticisms; but I must acknowledge my great debt to Mr. A. D. K. Owen, of P.E.P., for wholeheartedly putting his unrivalled knowledge of the British Social Services at my disposal.

JULIAN HUXLEY

Foreword

By Lord Horder, G.C.V.O.

THAT Democracy is not static but dynamic; that it is not a rigid and established order of things but is constantly changing with the changes that mark our personal, social and economic life; and that human progress and well-being are directly related to the degree to which this principle of vitality exists in a democratic nation—this is the author's theme in his present book.

It is true that Democracy connotes an attitude of mind on the part of an individual or a nation, but to be effective as an expression of personal or political faith it must be translated into action. In the piping times of peace the tempo is prone to be slow; with exigency in the saddle the pace quickens; the will to victory stirs us from our lethargy into alertness and performance.

Dr. Huxley marshals before us the very considerable contributions to the progress of civilisation which Democracy has recently made and is now making in this country. The array is both formidable and inspiring. The instances given spread over the whole field of human endeavour and are of a kind and extent to go far towards correcting our national self depreciation.

It is almost superfluous to add that by unique

FOREWORD

opportunity, by highly trained observation and by a masterly gift for interpretation Dr. Huxley is pre-eminently fitted for this very task and the result is one of his most readable books.

(HORDER)

DEMOCRACY MARCHES

I

The Unifying Effect of War

EARLY in 1940 I was nearing the end of a rather strenuous two months' tour over most of North America, during which I had made contact with a very wide range of American personalities—politicians, churchmen, scientists, film stars, business men, artists, journalists. Among the chief preoccupations of America I found were the supposedly imperialist and therefore anti-democratic aims of my own country, and the danger to democracy involved in waging war in the modern totalitarian way.

Since then, America has been thoroughly woken up to the fact that Britain is not fighting for its Empire but for its life, and that there are greater dangers to democracy than the fact of fighting for its continued existence, however great may be the temporary sacrifices of liberty involved. But I am not sure how much Americans realize, not merely how very lively the democratic spirit has remained here, but, still more, the remarkable fact that in some ways our democracy is actually evolving and progressing.

In October, when the night bombing of London was still both regular and intense, I persuaded a rather distinguished public servant to share the 'air-raid supper' which the German planes forced us to put at the unpleasant hour of 6.30, before going down to our basement shelter. After supper, my guest had to get back to his office. We put our tin hats on, I got my car out, and ran him down through streets which were, literally, all but deserted, owing to the violence of the raid and the barrage. On the way we began exchanging confidences. We both, it turned out, had been really frightened for a bit after the collapse of France. Visions of invasion, of being trapped like rats and unable to escape from these islands, of concentration camps (we both had been a good deal too liberal in public for the Gestapo's taste) had fixed themselves into our unwilling brains and produced unpleasant feelings from time to time in the pits of our stomachs. It hadn't made us less determined to fight, but it had been an additional horror to fight against. But then the horror had receded. It became clear not only that Britain could defend itself, but that a spirit of leadership, a sense of mission, was asserting itself in what had seemed a lethargic nation. What is more, that spirit of leadership was already looking ahead, beyond the war, to the peace. Change was in the air, and the British people were going to have something to say about the kind of change they wanted. And our final confession to each other, between the bangs and the bombs and under the hard white light of the parachute flares, was that, even though existence in

THE UNIFYING EFFECT OF WAR

London was very inconvenient, though waiting in a basement for the next bomb to fall was extremely unpleasant, though the ordinary pleasures of social life and entertainment were almost non-existent—all the same, neither of us would have been anywhere else for a very great deal. 'When I think we may really bring it off,' my friend said, and fell silent. But I knew what he was thinking. He was thinking that there was a chance for us not only to beat the Nazis, but to experience a revival of internal will and power which would once again give Britain a position of real leadership in the advance of civilization.

That somewhat exalted mood is over. With the passing of imminent danger, the British pass readily from heroics to grumbling. But it has left a real change in atmosphere, in the way the people at large are thinking.

And by people I don't mean just the little group of people with whom I happen to be intimate—I mean a surprising range of people, including, as well as those with so-called 'left' tendencies, much of the central backbone of the country, well-to-do business men, civil servants, even Conservative Cabinet Ministers.

What people are now thinking, and what many of them are publicly saying, is not merely that the war is irrevocably changing the framework of British life but that this is a good thing, and that we should make that transformation part of our war aims.

Naturally, they don't all agree as to just what the transformation ought to be; but there is general agreement that it must be towards something more democratic.

Perhaps it would be better to say that they have come to realize the fact that our pre-war democracy was, to put it mildly, very imperfect, and that its machinery was quite out of date when it comes to dealing with all the new problems that the modern world has sprung on it; and at the same time they have had the essential oneness of the British people, the solidarity of our society, forced home to their minds and hearts. And this simultaneous realization of these two facts has set them to thinking how the idea and practice of democracy might be and ought to be translated to suit present-day conditions.

Our democracy was imperfect in three main ways. First came the sense of insecurity, with consequent fear and anxiety, under which a majority of our people lived. Mass unemployment was the main visible sign of this. Then there was a lack of group feeling, a lack of cohesion in the community as a whole, and a lack of a deep sense of some purpose in life. And finally, there was our class system, with its glaring inequalities of power, wealth, and privilege. The combined effect was a sense of frustration, none the less haunting for often being unconscious. The very fact that democracy had succeeded in raising the average standard of living very considerably, but had not been able to cope with mass unemployment and economic insecurity, made things worse.

There has indeed been a tendency to exaggerate both our own faults, and the sense of frustration that we shared in some measure with every modern industrial community, including the U. S. A. After all, our unemployment figures never reached the United States level; and the feeling of frustration was much more acute in pre-Hitler Germany than over here. There has also been a tendency to forget our past achievements. Religious toleration, freedom of speech, the rights of association, a free press, universal education, the revitalization of local government, a big all-round programme of social services—these were no mean achievements of our democracy in the past; and they are still very far from having been neutralized by the new political and economic developments of the last few decades.

Let me remind the citizens of the United States who may be critical of our democracy of a few facts. To a much greater extent than over there, our local government is in the hands of representative bodies manned largely by working men and women. The Trade Union and Co-operative Movements not only play an important part in the industrial life of the country, but have become accepted as filling an essential role in our politics and administration. By means of old age and other pensions, and especially by our unemployment insurance system, we had made a very real attempt to cope with economic insecurity, which saved us from some of the worst consequences which citizens of the United States felt more acutely. Similarly our health insurance scheme was a very real attempt to cope with the problem of sickness. Our State system of education has made very great strides of recent years, especially in regard to secondary schools.

Health had rightly become linked with education in the various measures adopted for providing free or cheap milk and meals for undernourished children. In the huge problem of abolishing unhealthy and out-of-date living conditions by rehousing the people we have done really great things. With the aid of large-scale grants and a great deal of initiative and encouragement both from the central government and local authorities, we have in the last twenty years built over four and a half million houses—enough to provide new houses for over a third of our total population. The people of North America are just waking up to the fact that they are lagging behind us in these fields. Money talks: and it is an impressive fact that since 1900, the amount of money spent on our social services has increased tenfold per head of the population.

Later, I shall try to describe some of these past achievements much more in detail, and point out what new improvements are in the offing. Meanwhile, the last ten years had brought matters to a head. Insecurity, both economic and political, had increased beyond all previous measure, until the very idea of democracy was threatened.

People in general had not bothered their heads about all this in the years before the war; they were too busy trying to exist, or to patch up the decaying economic system and to keep pace with the activities of Mussolini, Hitler, and Stalin. But when it came to fighting for their lives, and for the life of the country, they were forced, almost against their will, to think about these things.

And meanwhile the war had also forced the various sections of the people to think about each other—both about each other's needs, and about the services they were receiving from and rendering to one another. Airmen, A.R.P. workers, fire-fighters, mine-sweepers—these, who had before been just ordinary people, were realized as vital elements in the country's united war effort; merchant seamen, factory workers, drivers of trains and buses, telephone girls, whose work had been taken for granted in time of peace, were heroes whose heroism had become indispensable to all the rest of us. Evacuation had sent the townsfolk into the homes of country people; bombing had brought all types and classes into contact; a new kind of community existence was developing in the air-raid shelters.

Yes, after all we were one body, though we had failed to realize the fact in peacetime. Was it partly because we had failed to realize this that there was so much uncertainty and frustration about? If we now tried to see what are the real implications of being a united society, of oneness and solidarity throughout the community, might we not as our first job have to make sure that fear and insecurity were removed from all those who used to live under their shadow? And if the sense of being part of a greater whole, the *Fraternity* aspect of the democratic picture, should really become an active force, would that not remove the frustration and aimlessness from people's lives, by giving them something to live for that was both concrete and bigger than themselves? Our democracy has been marching forward during the last century. There was a big spurt just before the last war, and another spurt after it. Now, it seems, we are on the verge of another big onward push.

II

The British Brand of Democracy

BEFORE going further, I must say a few words about British democracy in general, as opposed to democracy in other countries, like America. Americans are apt to think that democracy in Britain is rather a sham, because it differs in so many ways from American democracy, and especially because of our monarchy and our class system.

I suppose it is inevitable for the people of any particular country to think that their own ways are more natural, their own system somehow more right than the systems of other countries. It takes travel, or some knowledge of history, or both—together with a certain effort of mind—to realize that this need not be the case. Democracy, for example, is not in any way a fixed system. Any particular democracy is a particular attempt to realize the general democratic ideal. And that ideal is, historically speaking, something very recent. It is first of all the belief that individual human beings are what matter most—more than the State, or the total of national wealth, or anything else whatsoever. Then it is the belief in equality, not in the sense that everybody is alike or equally gifted, which is obviously untrue, but in the sense that everyone should have certain basic opportunities.

DEMOCRACY MARCHES

The European political theorists of the eighteenth century thought in terms of 'natural rights': the American Constitution speaks of 'life, liberty, and the pursuit of happiness.' Today we are more inclined to use phrases like privileges and opportunities. What each age has meant is that everyone should have an equal chance to a reasonable development as individual human beings, irrespective of accidents of birth or fortune. The democratic ideal is also the belief that governments should exist not only to benefit but to represent the people as a whole. So democracy, since it thus presupposes government by consent, implies tolerance; since it presupposes equality, implies equal opportunities; since it presupposes the ultimate value of individual men and women, implies freedom.

That is the democratic ideal. Actual democracies represent attempts at realizing this ideal. But, to date, all of them are still sadly imperfect; and they have pursued different methods in different countries.

Thus democracies can differ in two quite different ways. They can be more or less imperfect. There are democracies in which considerable sections of the people are not allowed to vote. That was so in Britain before the Reform Bill of 1832, and it still is so in the southern United States (for it makes no real difference whether people are disfranchised under the constitution, or in fact are simply not allowed to vote). Such democracies are obviously less perfect than those where there is real universal suffrage.

But besides differing on an up-and-down scale, they can also differ sideways, so to speak, just like different kinds of animals. A dogfish is a higher kind of animal than a jellyfish. But no one can say whether it is higher or lower than a lobster—its organization is quite different; it does the same kind of things, but in different ways. So with democracies. The American and British brands are both on about the same level of progress towards the ideal; but they are very different in their organization.

The chief difference lies in the British class system. Of course, in the United States colour and nationality to a certain degree take the place of class. On the whole, negroes and recent immigrants get fewer opportunities, in the same sort of way as the working classes in Britain get fewer opportunities. It is, of course, also true that, with the intense growth of industrialism in the United States, and with the closing of the frontier, a new class system, based mainly on money, but in part (in the East), on ancestry, is beginning to grow up —and doing so with rather alarming rapidity in some regions. But the British class system is much more rigid, and it is also historically ingrained, being a gradual evolution from the feudal system centuries back. In fact, the development of British society and institutions has almost always been gradual. It was this organic quality which Edmund Burke defended so eloquently against the theorists who wanted to imitate the French Revolution by making a clean sweep and starting again from as near scratch as possible. As he wrote, 'Society is indeed a contract . . . it is a partnership in all science; a partnership in all art; a partnership in every virtue and in all perfection. As the ends of such a partnership cannot be obtained in many generations, it becomes a partnership not only between those who are living, but between those who are living, those who are dead, and those who are to be born.' Burke, as usual, is being rhetorical; but his rhetoric clothes an important idea, the desirability of an organic society in general, and of an organic evolution where possible, as against a violent revolution. For the same reason, he upheld the class system of his time, but was careful to add that every society must contain machinery for change.

I am not attempting to make out that the British class system is the best way, or even a good way, of organizing a democracy. Later, I shall have a good deal to say about its evils and how far they have been, and may be further, got rid of. All I am here concerned with is to try to make clear that it is not incompatible with a reasonable amount of democracy (and also with a reasonably rapid progress towards more and better democracy), and that it has still, and has had in the past, quite a number of merits. Its merits are orderliness and a sense that everyone has a job of work to do for the community; among the more privileged, a sense of duty towards society and towards those who happen to be less fortunate; a very considerable amount of freedom within the boundaries set by the system; sufficient fluidity to give talent a reasonable chance to rise, and to allow new classes, as they become important, to take their share of leadership and responsibility; plenty of opportunity for people to take part in their own local government; and still more opportunity for them to form voluntary associations to look after their own interests. This is a very important aspect of democracy; for, to quote again from Burke, 'To be attached to the subdivision, to love the little platoon, is the first principle (the germ as it were) of public affections.'

About the monarchy I need not say much. Everyone, even in the republican United States, should, I hope, realize that being a king means something very different to George VI from what it did to George III. The British King is no longer an autocrat, and indeed, has lost almost every vestige of political power. He is now, in one sense, only a symbol of the unity of the nation, and of the Empire. But symbols can be very important, and our twentieth-century kings are very active, hardworking, and useful members of the community, focussing loyalties, giving the necessary personal touch to the vast impersonal machinery of a modern state, and infinitely more democratic than your Führers or your Duces, with their bodyguards and their pomp. The American President too is a democratic personal head; but Presidents are also members of political parties, and some of the bitterness of politics inevitably hangs around them. There is something to be said for a personal head who is above politics, who succeeds to his position by virtue of inheritance, and not by having to get himself elected, who cannot, save for rare constitutional reasons, be got rid of, and who embodies an immemorial tradition and ritual.

There is naturally another side to the picture. The traditional side of the monarchy can be overdone, and may make the ritual too much a survival of the past, too little representative of today: some people felt that about our last Coronation ceremonies. It is difficult for the existence of a court not to encourage a certain not very desirable snobbery. Certain traditional vested interests may manage to entrench themselves under the sheltering wing of monarchy.

Similarly with the British class system. It undoubtedly stimulates snobbery. Many among the privileged classes come to take their privileged position for granted, and rather forget their obligations of service. In small communities like the village, the local bigwigs may easily become petty tyrants instead of real leaders or public servants. The fear of losing privileges may, consciously or unconsciously, generate hostility or overbearingness towards the so-called lower classes, while conversely jealousy may make the under-privileged bitter and resentful. Most important of all, the class system does mean a considerable deprivation of equal opportunity; and this is a very real negation of the democratic ideal.

All the same, British democracy manages to work reasonably well, in spite of obvious and numerous defeats. The best proof of that is that our system has, in the last hundred years, become more, and not less, democratic, in spite of all the undemocratic handicaps it has inherited from the past, and all the new anti-democratic burdens that the *laisser-faire* period managed to pile on its back.

I shall have more to say about this slow but steady progress towards fuller democracy. Here, let me end with a brief picture of how democracy means something real to the average Englishman today. First, Britain is politically democratic. There is real universal suffrage, for men and women alike. There is much less intimidation of voters than takes place in various American states, and much less political graft. This is particularly true of city government: the general record of the London County Council is must pleasanter to contemplate than that of the New York City Administration, for instance. We have never had any anti-democratic organization so powerful as the Ku Klux Klan during its brief but unenviable prominence, nor any political machines so ruthless and corrupt as those of certain American States, or as Tammany in its heyday.

Local government has, on the whole, been in the control of local people, duly elected to represent the balance of local interests; the small political boss has never played so unpleasant a role here as in parts of the U.S.A., and local government is largely in the hands of the working class. The mayor of a small city, or the members of a Borough Council, are just as likely to be working men as aristocrats or rich merchants or business men.

Britain's legal system is reasonably democratic: the high cost of going to law is its only serious handicap. There had been very little corruption, either among judges or police, which is more than some regions in the United States can say of themselves; and racketeering has never been able to become a major scandal in this country. The Civil Service is appointed by the democratic system of examination; the undemocratic 'spoils' system has never played the part it has done in the United States. Then we must remember that Britain was a pioneer of religious freedom, as well as of political freedom. The growth of nonconformity, with its myriads of active, independent, and earnest congregations, played a great part in encouraging individual independence and all kinds of crusading movements. Democracy can come alive in various ways, and one of them is by having a sense of mission about various democratic ideals. The British anti-slavery movement is a notable example of this; and the same sense of crusading for freedom on a world-wide scale animated much of our foreign policy during the nineteenth century.

The Protestant tradition of independence also found embodiment in all sorts of organizations for self-help. Our British Trade Unions, our innumerable Friendly Societies with their mutual insurance schemes, and later, our Co-operative Movement, all came into being as vigorous expressions of British democracy. The British idea of individual liberty is crystallized in the phrase 'The Englishman's home is his castle.' In addition, press, speech and opinion are as free with us as in any country in the world. The speakers at Hyde Park Corner, letting off steam about religion, or Communism, or Fascism, or any other 'ism' they like, are a symbol of that aspect of democracy. Even Americans seem to find it extraordinary that such violent and revolutionary utterances are so freely tolerated, Sunday after Sunday, in the very centre of the Empire.

In its labour relations Britain has, on the whole, been more democratic than the United States. Our strikes have never been marred by such violence as in America, nor turned into miniature civil wars; the military power has not been so much used to overawe labour; and we have not suffered so much from illegal or extra-legal *vigilante* organizations.

Collective bargaining and political Trades Unionism are among the useful machinery by which British democracy has come to express itself.

As regards education, elementary education is free and universal, secondary education is cheap and of high standard, and, after many years, University education has become pretty thoroughly democratized. Voluntary effort is very prominent in this field and works on the whole in a democratic direction. Our educational system may be class-ridden, but it partly compensates for this by its extreme variety and the freedom from regimented uniformity which it enjoys.

We still have great inequality of wealth, though with us taxation destroys a considerably greater amount of that inequality than is the case in America; but the remarkable growth of our social services at least ensures that nobody shall fall below a certain minimum standard of life, that unemployment and sickness shall not spell destitution, and that the stigma of receiving charity or poor relief has been replaced by pensions and other benefits which men and women can accept as rights without any loss of self-respect.

Finally, British democracy in its imperial aspect has made one great invention—that of the Commonwealth of free and equal Dominions, bound together by common values and ideas instead of by compulsion or even by a formal constitution. The granting of self-government to South Africa after the Boer War, and the acceptance of Eire's neutrality in this war, are good examples of the democratic spirit at work in international relations.

Summing up, I think it is fair to say that the average Englishman has had the sense of being reasonably free to do and say what he likes, of being able to express his political views freely and fairly effectively, of being free to organize with others to stand up for his rights and interests, of belonging to a country which, on the whole, has consistently stood for freedom, of being given a reasonable opportunity to make something worth while out of his individual life. And that is a real form of democracy, if very far from a perfect one. Of late years that sense has been somewhat shaken by economic insecurity and the threat of war looming over Europe. But he is now very much determined that the freedoms and opportunities he has achieved in the past shall not be lost, as has been shown during the war by the many protests that have been successfully made, both within and without Parliament, whenever the Government has gone too far in curtailing the safeguards of liberty for its citizens; and this determination is yet another expression of the democratic spirit.

III

The British Social Services

DEMOCRACY in Britain, for all its faults, has slowly but steadily progressed during the past century or so. To understand that process, it must be described against the general background of social trends.

During the Victorian era the continued growth of large towns steadily made Britain more of an urban civilization, but the community sense tended to decrease among the town-dwellers, and precious little grew up in the way of urban culture, or even of real urban social life, except in London or among the well-to-do. In large measure, the place of real culture eventually came to be taken by mass entertainment, that of active sport either by mass watching of sport or by the excitements of betting. During the twentieth century, much of the nation's leisure was given over to mass-produced spectator passivity. The result of these tendencies was that the mass of the people eventually came to feel more and more like mere human atoms, with fewer outlets for creative or shared social activities.

In the economic field, real wages went steadily up, but meanwhile big business in various forms— monopolies, combines, multiple-shop systems, and so forth—tended to replace ever more of the small enterprises characteristic of the earlier stages of the industrial revolution. Here again, the result was less personal contact—in this case between worker and employer—and an increasing sense of being at the mercy of blind economic processes. Finally, the full effects of *laisser-faire* individualism were everywhere making themselves felt—sprawling ugly towns, none of them complete without their slums, the development of a large proletariat, recurrent slumps and unemployment, the growth of vested interests entrenched behind the sacred profit motive. Prosperity was increasing, but so were awkward problems, and finally, after the last war, even prosperity failed and insecurity became the dominant mood.

But British democracy was not swamped by these difficulties, though some of them were threats to its very existence. It answered the challenge by producing what, in retrospect, we must agree was a remarkable system of social services. The orthodox Victorian view of the State's job in national life was that it should do as little as possible. Foreign policy was, of course, its affair, and the Army and Navy. But otherwise its concern was merely to keep the ring for the free play of individual enterprise. That meant being responsible for law and order—but beyond that, as little meddling as might be. However, events were too strong for theory, and the State was forced to take a hand, first in preventing various social abuses and later in organizing various community services: and so the *laisser-faire*, keep-the-ring State of the 1840's was gradually converted into the social service State which is in process of being born in the 1940's.

People with tidy minds classify the social services under five main heads. First come those services which are hardly social at all in the strict sense, but are concerned with the physical needs of civilization, such as water-supply, refuse removal, or drainage. We may call these the environmental services. Then there is social assistance—the helping of people who otherwise would be destitute. This includes what we used to call Poor Relief, and all the manifold activities of the Assistance Board. Next we have the social insurance services. These are really a form of compulsory self-help. People are required to make regular contributions to funds for such purposes as sickness benefits, old-age pensions, or unemployment benefits, the rest of the cost being borne by the State and the employer jointly.

Fourthly, there are what may be called the constructive community services, in which specialized institutions are created for the use of the community, and special professional skill put at its service. Health services, education, and employment exchanges are examples of these. And finally, we have subsidized consumption. This means that the community provides part or all of the cost of various essentials of healthy and civilized life which are beyond the reach of people with low incomes, but are regarded as necessary for national fitness. Housing subsidies or the provision of cheap or free milk for young children and nursing mothers are examples of this.

Almost all of these, except some of the environmental services, had their origin in voluntary effort. At the beginning of the modern period of history, about the beginning of the 1500's, the powers of the Church and the medieval Guilds broke down, and the new ferment of individual enterprise brought new prosperity but also widespread distress. Pious men founded almshouses for the poor and aged, hospitals for the sick, schools for the poor scholar. But benevolence proved not to be enough, and in the seventeenth and eighteenth centuries hundreds of organizations for mutual assistance sprang up all over the country—friendly societies, burial societies, insurance clubs, and the like.

Quite early, however, the State was forced to step in. Some problems were too urgent and too big for private benevolence or voluntary co-operation. Water-supply in towns has from the beginning been a public concern, even if it only took the form of public wells or fountains. Sanitation too soon came under public regulation; the Act for the rebuilding of London after the Great Fire of 1666 contained a number of provisions about the construction of sewers. The State was also soon forced to undertake public assistance. The rise of the wool trade in the fifteenth and sixteenth centuries led to the wholesale enclosure of arable land for sheep, and the country became filled with 'rogues and vagabonds' —poor landless men vainly trying to find a living in the towns or to pick one up by petty thieving in the countryside. This problem gave rise to a whole series of local enactments, which in 1601 culminated in our first national system of poor relief.

However, it took another major upset of the country's economic life to bring about public social services on a large scale. By the 1830's or thereabouts, the industrial revolution had again brought a sudden great increase in national prosperity, but this was again coupled with great distress for certain sections of the people. At the same time the growth of science and invention had produced appalling problems such as the too rapid growth of factories and big towns, but at the same time had begun to hold out hopes of solving them.

The history of the social services during the nineteenth century is a fascinating story if properly told: and also an instructive one, showing both the defects and the advantages of the democratic system under *laisser faire*. The chief defect was that it has almost always taken something serious to get any important change effected—some gross abuse like children employed on twelve-hour night-shifts in what Blake called the 'dark Satanic mills,' some major disaster like prolonged mass unemployment. The chief merit was that things did eventually get done, which was not the case under oppressive undemocratic systems like the *ancien régime* in eighteenth-century France, or Tsarist Russia. The fact that people were free to criticize and free to found private organizations for the relief of distress or the remedying of abuses, always eventually led to the problems being tackled on a national scale.

A further merit of a democratic system is that once any decisive step is taken in a democratic direction, further steps seem to become inevitable; the process acquires a momentum. For instance, once the State, in the famous Factory Act of 1833, had made it its business to protect children against the evils of excessive and unsuitable labour in the cotton mills, it really became inevitable that it would extend the protection to other industries, to adult women and to men. This was the germ out of which there could not but grow the elaborate provisions we now have for regulating hours of work, ventilation and lighting in factories, truck payments, dangerous trades.

In just the same way the setting up of a State system of elementary schools inevitably spelt the steady development of public education until it comprised secondary schools and penetrated the Universities. The elementary schooling of 1870, in spite of long hours, large classes, overcrowded schoolrooms, poor teachers and unsatisfactory curriculum, contained in embryo the spacious schools and enlightened teaching of today, and, under a democratic system, the one could not fail to develop into the other.

But the best way to visualize what the British social services are doing today is to describe their effect in terms of an ordinary man's life in the years just before the war. Think of a typical wage-earner —a young married man doing semi-skilled work in a factory, or a bus driver, or a shop assistant. He lives in a town where the public authorities see to it that drainage and street cleaning are so efficient that most people never think about them at all, where the borough council removes refuse, where he is protected against disease and short measure by food and shop inspectors. If he is lucky, he has secured a house on a municipal housing estate, which means that public money has been expended to allow of low rents. If he falls sick, under our National Health Insurance system he gets free treatment and free medicines from his panel doctor; and if his illness lasts any length of time, he receives cash payments too.

Meanwhile his wife is expecting a baby. If she is wise, she will go to one of the ante-natal clinics provided by the local authority, where she can be properly examined and advised and, if necessary, given suitable foods. When the time comes for the baby to be born, she has a choice between calling in a trained midwife belonging to the public midwifery service, or going into a public maternity ward at a hospital. Later, a health visitor will come to her home to advise on the baby's health and care, and the mother will almost certainly have the chance of attending an infant welfare centre, where the baby will be regularly weighed, examined, treated for minor ailments, and milk provided if need be. Later, if she is lucky she will have access to one of the nursery schools for children under 5, though there are all too few of these at present. In any case, when the little boy is 5, he will begin his compulsory schooling. During his time at an elementary school he will enjoy the advantages of the school medical system. This means thorough medical examination and treatment, free or at a nominal charge, for minor illnesses, defects of teeth and eyes, adenoids and tonsils. In many cases he will also be seen by one of the members of a voluntary care committee, who make it their business to follow up the school medical examination by visits to the child's home.

Meanwhile let us suppose that there has been a slump in trade, and the father has been thrown out of work. While employed he will have been paying his tenpence a week to the Unemployment Insurance scheme. Now he gets the benefit—thirty shillings a week for himself and an extra four shillings for his boy.

Unfortunately the depression continues, and so does his unemployment. After six months (or longer if he has been very regular in paying his weekly contributions) his right to unemployment insurance benefit lapses. But there is a second line of defence: he can apply for unemployment assistance. This is not a right, but a form of relief, and is assessed in relation to need. An official of the Assistance Board will investigate the man's circumstances, and assess the grant accordingly. This 'Means Test,' as it is usually called, has caused much friction and ill-feeling, and an Act has just been passed in Parliament which will get rid of a good deal of the trouble. Meanwhile, as unemployment benefit, and usually unemployment assistance, are considerably less than normal wages, the family's standard of living inevitably goes down somewhat. But the school medical service sees to it that if the child's health is likely to suffer, he will be given free milk and, in most areas, a free midday meal. Even boots and clothing will be provided free for the children of really needy parents.

All the time that he has been out of work, the father was registered at his local Employment Exchange, and, being an enterprising fellow, he has also gone to a Ministry of Labour unemployed training centre to be trained for another occupation and at last he gets the offer of a job. Unfortunately the region where he lives has become a chronically depressed area and the job is in another part of the country. But he can get the family's railway fare paid there, and a grant towards the cost of removal—and so he moves off to take up active work again elsewhere.

Unfortunately his wife has developed tuberculosis.

Luckily he now finds himself in a region where the local authority maintains sanatoria, and after six months there, she recovers her health.

The child is growing up and turns out to be an intelligent boy. So at the age of 11 he successfully takes an examination which qualifies him to go on to a secondary school till he is 16 or 17, instead of staying on in an elementary school and finishing his education at 14 or 15. His father is now earning good wages again and decides that he can manage the small fees which are payable. This turns out to be a good investment, for the lad eventually wins a scholarship which enables him to go on to the University. His education there is subsidized not only by the scholarship he has earned through his ability but by Government and local grants, which make up nearly half the total income of British Universities.

Under the various Old Age Pensions schemes, the man and his wife, when he is 65 and she 60, will draw thirty-two shillings a week, provided their resources do not exceed a stipulated amount. The social services touch his life from the cradle to the grave.

One final point. The fears which have often been expressed that the social services would undermine people's sense of personal responsibility have proved to be quite unfounded. This is demonstrated by the fact that small savings have enormously increased during what may be called the social service period, since 1910 or thereabouts.

IV

Social Service and Democracy

I HAVE given a summary picture of the gradual growth of our elaborate system of social services, up to their present high level, where they touch the life of the common man at every point from birth to old age. But I can almost hear some of my readers saying, 'That is all very well, but why call it Democracy? Has not every advanced country done something similar, the totalitarian states as much as the democracies?' That is perfectly valid. Social services dealing with unemployment, health, housing, education, maternity, security in old age, and so forth, are necessary for the working of any modern industrial nation. In some fields, in fact, the totalitarians have pushed further ahead with their social services than we or any democratic country. This is notably so with leisure and recreation. The Nazi movement *Kraft durch Freude* or 'Strength through Enjoyment', which itself is an improved version of the Fascist organization *Dopo Lavoro* or 'After Working Hours,' was in its earlier years a very great success. It provided recreation and, what is equally important, travel for German working men and women on a large scale. It rescued them from feeling just isolated individuals, and provided social outlets for their leisure and their pleasures.

They felt that the State was taking a personal interest in their lives and their happiness. Many observers think that *Kraft durch Freude*, at least for the large section of the German workers which was not strongly politically-minded, was the greatest single reason for welcoming or at least accepting the Nazi regime.

The other great totalitarian country, Russia, also has very efficient leisure services. Not only is elaborate provision made in the parks of big cities for recreation of all sorts, including intellectual recreation, but the remarkable system of rest-houses gives quite new opportunities for healthy and happy holidays. Some of the rest centres are close to big towns and are meant for short holidays, but for longer holidays workers get free travel to special holiday centres, such as the lovely Black Sea coast. This seems to have produced a major revolution in social habits and in sense of well-being.

No, we must face the fact that social services are not necessarily democratic. The democratic trend is one thing, the social service trend is something quite separate and different. The modern social service trend was in its origin a consequence, apparently an inevitable consequence, of the growth of capitalist industrialism. It has passed through several well-marked stages. At the outset it was mainly concerned with the remedying of particular gross abuses, such as child labour, or particular gross deficiencies, such as popular ignorance or the lack of proper drainage in big cities. But during the present century it has on the whole set itself a more general task—of patching the social gaps left by the *laisser-faire* system, especially as regards security—security against sickness, against old age, against unemployment and so forth.

When new social services have been introduced in a democratic country, they have naturally tended to fit in with democratic ideas, and often to make its system more democratic than before. But in a totalitarian country, they have, equally naturally, been used to promote greater national efficiency and greater subordination of the individual to the party and the State.

However, totalitarian countries are no longer *laisser-faire*. Their very existence is a symptom of a new stage in the social service movement—a trend towards something more positive, towards a type of State in which social instead of economic motives are dominant.

As Peter Drucker has so vividly set forth in his book *The End of Economic Man*, the rise of dictatorship, notably in Germany, was made possible by the sense of frustration and despair which seized upon ever-increasing numbers of people. The economic age, of individualism and *laisser-faire* capitalism, had promised all men freedom and equality. But the political freedom of the vote had been swallowed up in the tyranny of the party machine. Economic liberty had turned out to be an illusion;

the common man came to realize, first, that he was in a certain real sense a wage-slave, and then, that both he and his employers were prisoners in the clutch of huge impersonal economic forces which seemed beyond anybody's control. And then, as a result of the economic age, equality was farther off than ever; the old inequality of birth and inherited privilege had merely been replaced by a new and in some ways more violent inequality of wealth and power.

Finally, there was fraternity, the last of the three torches of hope which the French Revolution had kindled to illuminate the succeeding age. Nothing very much had ever been done to make that a reality. Indeed the very spirit of individualism which had been the driving force of the industrial revolution had made any attempts in that direction suspect. The nineteenth century believed that the free play of economic forces, working through individual enterprise, was bound to produce the quickest results and the best in the long run. If the system also produced unemployment and bankruptcies and other miseries, these were the inevitable price to be paid for progress. To make fraternity a reality would mean interfering in a big way with the forces working for progress, and so the attempt must be resisted, or at most tolerated as a means of patching up the economic machine.

The result was that the civilized world felt let down by the system under which it lived. Increasing numbers of people lost hope and found it more and more difficult to realize, or even to conceive, any truly satisfying aim in life, whether a personal aim or a shared social aim. And when finally, as in Germany in the early 1930's, the economic basis of existence began to collapse, the loss of hope and purpose turned to active despair. Despair clutched at anything which promised a way out—the more irrational the better, as despair itself is irrational, and cannot conceive of being rescued save by magic or miracle. It was on this wave that the Nazis were able to grasp power, with their self-contradictory promises of salvation for everyone—big business and the little man, landless peasants and great landowners, the army patriot and the peaceful citizen, the revolutionary and the anti-Bolshevik.

But to begin to make a job of their new system of National Socialism and to honour a reasonable number of their promises, the Nazis were inevitably forced to organize the social services in a new way. Instead of the State regarding the social services as palliatives, as so many means of patching up the defects that were appearing in the individualist capitalist system, they began to use them as essential parts of a new kind of system, one in which every aspect of social life was organized and unified. Social ideals were put in the foreground, and economic ones relegated to a secondary place. The State became (among other much less desirable things) an active and positive instrument for supplying social services to society at large.

It is of course true that the Nazi system is radically anti-democratic, with power as its only final aim, so that the real purpose of the Nazis' social services is to make the German State more powerful, not to give greater opportunities for fuller life and development to individual Germans. But this does not make it any less true that it is a positive instrument of social service, and, what is more, a very efficient one.

However, it is also true that democratic states may turn themselves into active instruments of social service. This transformation has to a considerable extent been more or less fully accomplished by some of the small democracies of Europe —the Scandinavian countries and Switzerland. One of the main immediate jobs before the large and influential democracies, such as Britain and the United States, is to combine the democratic trend with the social service trend in a really satisfactory way. This means building up a new kind of State, a new sort of machinery of Government, one of whose main aims will be to serve its citizens in all the fields where individual or voluntary action is not enough, while at the same time giving them real freedom and real equality of opportunity: we in this country have already taken a number of separate steps in this direction, but we still need to formulate the idea clearly and to proclaim it as our goal. To be sure of keeping the essence of democracy, the State must not frown on individual initiative and voluntary organizations, but encourage them and use them to the greatest possible extent. It must not stamp out freedom of thought and opinion, but must deliberately protect them. It must not try to regiment the whole population into a single machine obeying the will of the gang behind the State, but must encourage them in creative criticism and liberty of association and independent action. It must aim at variety, not uniformity; at tolerance, not blind acceptance of dogma; at willing co-operation, not obedience; at Government through consent, not through force and violence.

To make a thorough job of turning the State into an active instrument of social service, obviously implies a real revolution in political thought, a radical recasting of the idea of Government—why it exists, and how it should work. Later, I shall have more to say on this, and on the way the separate social services are likely to develop once this fusion of the democratic idea with the idea of the social service State becomes not only practical politics, but a main aim of our democratic policy. Here I will end with a brief picture of a change that has already taken place in Britain, largely as the result of our social services in the past, and one that is also a step in the process of changing over our national life from an economic to a social basis. I will try to put the change in terms of types of human beings, rather than in general terms.

In the latter half of the nineteenth century, and up to the last war, the ruling class was the propertied class. Though the majority of rich men had made their money in business, they tended to buy estates and settle down as country gentlemen, so assimilating themselves to the tradition of the pre-industrial age, when land was the most important form of property, and the ruling class was drawn almost entirely from the landed aristocracy and gentry. The rich, in return for the privileges they enjoyed, on the whole rendered a good deal of service to the community, whether in public life, or in various forms of charity or idealistic enterprise. *Noblesse oblige* was the symbol of this spirit at its best. The labouring classes, on the other hand, were gradually coming to organize themselves in Trade Unions and co-operatives, to achieve a certain number of privileges for themselves, and to build up a solid foundation of economic rights, so as to get rid of the need for receiving charity and poor relief. In business, competition was the order of the day; individual enterprise was the quality most highly valued, and mere success was largely the measure of public esteem. For business and for economic theory alike, labour was just a commodity; and labour responded by regarding capital as its political enemy. The country had two sharply distinct systems of education. One was available only to the rich, or, with the aid of scholarships, to the sons of poor clergymen and other professional men. This served for the education of gentlemen—a term much in use in a class sense at that time—and for the training of the ruling and administrative classes. The other was given to the poor. It was quite different in content, and, for all but a tiny handful, stopped much earlier. It was provided partly for charitable and religious motives, but largely to turn out more efficient and also more docile factory workers, clerks, artisans, and agricultural labourers.

But today, as a result of changes in our economic organization, combined with educational developments, a new class has arisen. The head and front of it are the skilled people—technicians, school teachers, trained nurses, local government officials, second-grade civil service clerks—all the people who fill the role of NCO's, and junior officers in industry, management, training and all the complicated business of a modern technological nation. In this war, the type and symbol of them are the sergeant-pilot and the aircraft mechanic. They are, by and large, the product not of the rich man's system of education, but of the secondary schools, which have developed as the crown of the poor man's educational system. The existence of the secondary school has also meant that the children of the less skilled members of this intermediate class—such as shopkeepers and tradesmen and builders and small farmers—are also getting the opportunity of a good education.

This new class is now one of the most important sections of the community. The people in it are not property owners, or only in a very small way. Nor are they 'Labour' either in the economic or in the political sense, with its traditional hostility to capital. Their assets are their skill and the key functions they perform.

In relation to this class, the tradition of charity has broken down, and is being replaced by the principle of service. They are above receiving charity, but are not in a position to dispense with it. The war has forced them out of their shells, so to speak, into positions where they are not only rendering invaluable services, but are beginning to be conscious of doing so. Instead of carrying on in the narrow groove of making a small living with the hope of a small rise in standard for their children, they are realizing that their job is a national service, and that national service is another and more satisfying way of looking at their jobs.

What is more, the idea of service as a duty is beginning to replace the idea of voluntary effort and charity in the higher economic classes also. They too are finding their outlets in national jobs—A.R.P., Home Guard, the Auxiliary Fire Service—and sharing their service as equals with men from every other class.

This marks the first stage in the transformation

of our economic society into a social one, and is an essential step towards the active Social Service State which is also democratic. We must see that this new backbone of ours, this skilled but propertyless class, gets the political opportunities it deserves; and we must make sure that the idea of national service shall persist, in some form or other, into the peace. That will explode the present political system, which is really a myth surviving from an earlier age, with its division of parties into the two hostile camps of property and capital versus labour and a jealous proletariat, and it will make it possible for people to think of themselves as serving members of a living and growing community, instead of competing atoms trapped in a blind and impersonally malignant economic system.

V

Social Standards

IT is not easy to plan out a system of positive social service which will be both efficient and democratic. If you think too much about efficiency, you are quite liable to sacrifice some degree of individual freedom, or of personal initiative. If you think too much about democratic liberty and equality, you may find that you have interfered with the efficiency of your social service machinery. In any case, as large-scale social service is an enormous and difficult business, you may find yourself landed with a cumbrous bureaucracy in which both efficiency and personal liberty are suffocated in red tape.

All the same, there are certain general principles for a democratic Social Service State, and in certain fields the broad lines of them are already beginning to emerge in practice. The most basic of those principles, it seems to me, is that of minimum social standards.

Here let me make a brief digestion into scientific history. Just thirty years ago a Cambridge biochemist called Hopkins conclusively proved that the ordinary foodstuffs which physiology said were enough to keep you in health—the starches, sugars, fats and proteins—would not in point of fact do so. Other substances were necessary—only in tiny traces, but nevertheless necessary. Several other workers had guessed or hinted at something of the sort, but Hopkins was the first to prove it. Now he is Sir Gowland Hopkins, past President of the Royal Society, and what he discovered was the first of what are now called the 'accessory food factors'; they include all the vitamins from A to K, and various mineral salts as well.

What has this got to do with the future of democracy? The answer is clear enough. After all, the opportunity of a healthy and fully developed body is the primary and basic service which a social service democracy owes to its members. And, through all the mass of scientific and clinical work which sprang from this discovery of Hopkins', we are now able, for the first time in history, to set up standards by which we can measure whether people are getting the minimum physiological diet—all the different kinds of foodstuffs required to give them that healthy and well-developed body.

Appetite, common-sense, feeling full and satisfied after your meals—none of these is a safe guide. It is scientific research alone which has enabled us to lay down the standard. If that standard is not kept, and there is a deficiency of any of the necessary foodstuffs, people will have less physical and mental energy, they will suffer from slight symptoms which a bigger deficiency will convert into this or that definite disease, they will be less resistant than they might be to infection, and, if they are still children,

SOCIAL STANDARDS

they will not grow as tall or as strong as they ought to.

We can also measure how far any group of people fall short of reaching this standard; and when this is done, some very surprising and disturbing facts emerge. In Britain about 40 per cent. of our forty million people are not getting this minimum healthy diet: something like half of these are being definitely under-nourished, the other half only slightly. The figure does not pretend to be exact—it may be as much as half the population, or as low as a third, but it is undoubtedly very high. In the U.S.A. it is not quite so high, but is still somewhere between 25 and 40 per cent.

That would be bad enough; but there is worse to come. If we take children only, then the proportion of the seriously under-nourished is almost doubled, and that of the slightly under-nourished is increased by some 50 per cent. Out of every ten boys and girls under 15, only about three are getting adequate food for them to realize their full birthright of health and strength. How does this come about? In the first place, families are not all of the same size. In this country, about five-sixths of the families which contain children under 15 are one- or no-child families. Those with two or more children are thus only one-sixth of the total number of families: but they include about half the total number of children. And secondly, it is a sad but unescapable fact that, under our present system, children are an economic drag. As one well-known social reformer has put it, children are the greatest single cause of poverty in Britain today. A recent survey in an industrial area showed that families including three or more children under 15 amounted to only a fifth of all the working-class families; but of families below the poverty line, they made up three-quarters.

It is an appalling thought that about three-quarters of the future citizens of one of the world's most prosperous and powerful countries are growing up less big, less strong, less healthy, less energetic, less disease-resistant, than by rights they ought to be.

It follows that if our first principle is that there are minimum standards of physical existence which a democracy ought to assure to its members, our second is that we shall only be able to manage this if we take the family as the unit target, so to speak, for the social services.

In some form or other family allowances have got to come, or else large numbers of children will continue to be deprived of their full birthright of health. The simplest way would probably be to issue every mother with coupons entitling her to a free (or very cheap) supply of certain essential protective foods for herself and for each child. We long ago made a beginning of this in our school medical system, by providing free or cheap milk and meals for the very poor children; this has been taken a step further during the war, and the scheme has been extended by providing cheap or free milk to expectant mothers, and to children under five. Over two and a half million mothers and babies are already taking advantage of this service.

Some people object that this will ruin the sense of parental responsibility; however, all the experience we have is to the contrary. For instance, the fact that unemployment and sickness insurance and old age pensions are now provided, has not discouraged the practice of saving, but has actually stimulated it. Others prefer to believe that the people would at once begin to breed like rabbits. But this seems a wholly imaginary fear, since under no conceivable system of family allowances could it actually *pay* to have more children.

But I must go back to the question of standards. It is not only in diet that you can set up measurable standards. You can do so for various other aspects of health also, by utilizing the published figures on death-rates and disease-rates. This again has been made possible by science, though in rather a different way. It has been made possible partly through the great advances in medicine and public health during the past seventy or eighty years (which in their turn have depended on scientific discoveries like the discovery of the cause of infectious disease by bacteria) and partly by the large-scale use of statistics, which is itself one aspect of scientific method.

Thus you can set up measurable standards in

relation to infant mortality. Some babies are bound to die before they are a year old. In advanced countries like New Zealand, the number is only 3 out of every hundred; in Britain as a whole it still is about 6; in Glasgow, over 10; in tropical Africa anything from 25 to 50! So with general mortality. It ought to be below 10 per thousand; in Britain it is still over 12. So with maternal mortality: a reasonable standard is about 2 deaths for every thousand confinements. So with various diseases. Deaths from tuberculosis should not, if we applied our modern knowledge, be above 25 or 30 per hundred thousand; deaths from diphtheria should not be above 3 or 4: in Britain, the rates are over 70 and over 8 respectively.

When it comes to housing, our standards will be more arbitrary, but need not be less measurable. So many rooms for a family of a given size, so much cubic space, a bath, various elementary conveniences—we can lay down a minimum for health and decent living. The minimum laid down for working-class housing by a Government Committee in 1918 was as follows: a living room, a separate kitchen, three bedrooms, a bathroom and water-closet, all with windows to the open air, and a ventilated larder; the minimum floor space to be 750 square feet. It will take a considerable time to achieve this in all working-class housing, but it would help if it were officially set up as a national standard. Similarly with clothing; there is a minimum of warmth and protection to be expected from clothes and boots.

And we can extend the principle of standards to the mind as well as the body. The most obvious and necessary is a standard of education. We can set two sorts of standards here. First, a minimum standard below which no one is allowed to fall, in the shape of so many years of elementary education in such and such subjects. And secondly, and in a way even more important, a standard of equal opportunity for all, to ensure that no boy or girl is deprived of the chance of climbing to the top of the educational ladder through poverty or the accidents of birth.

There are also standards of economic security. During the recent past, the sense of insecurity has been the greatest single cause, both of individual anxiety and frustration, and of social instability and unrest. A social service State must see to it that it gives to all its citizens minimum standards of security against ill-health, against unemployment, against widowhood, against old age. A man cannot be a good citizen nor do himself justice as an individual if he lives in a nightmare of frustration and anxiety about losing his job, if he has only a bleak and unprovided old age to look forward to, if he is afraid to be treated for ill-health for fear of the economic effects on his family. But do not let us forget that the final step must be to provide security against unemployment by getting rid of unemployment itself, to provide security against ill-health by making positive good health the rule. And of course there are also standards of civil liberty. In Britain those have been fairly well established—we have quite high standards for freedom of the press, for freedom of belief, for freedom of assembly and of individual opinion, for freedom of the person against arbitrary arrest or secret police action, for freedom from torture or other cruel methods. But it is still necessary to guard these jealously against any encroachment.

We have gone a considerable way towards securing various of these standards in practice; but as yet we have not set about the business in any coherent way. To do this we need first of all to recognize that there are measurable standards of physical and mental health, of physical and mental development, and of freedom from economic anxiety. And then we must recognize that it is the business of a democratic country to ensure, with the aid of its social services, that none of its people, grown-ups or children, are prevented from reaching those standards by forces outside their control.

We may thus say that a 'People's Minimum' will be the charter of the new type of State which combines democracy with positive social service.

VI

Health in a Democratic Britain

IN EARLIER chapters I have said something about the general trends to be seen in the development of social services in a democracy. How they originate as efforts to get rid of some abuse or piece of inefficiency so gross that the public conscience cannot tolerate it, or some social misery on too large a scale to be disregarded. How these efforts usually are voluntary to begin with, but soon get supplemented or taken over by the State; how later the social services grow into a fairly complete system for patching up the framework of *laisser-faire* society, and still later turn into deliberate and comprehensive instruments of positive action; how the idea of a living and organic society replaces the belief in *laisser-faire*; and, finally, how in such a society the service aspect begins to crystallize out round the principle of a national minimum, based on definite and measurable standards, to be aimed at for every individual in the community.

I would like to illustrate these rather general statements by describing something of the actual history of some of the English social services, and the way in which very recent developments are leading them on to their logical conclusion.

Let me begin with health. Our present health

services, in the widest sense of that word, have grown out of several different roots. In the first place, there was the need to prevent filth and pollution and consequent epidemics, out of which sprang our modern system of sanitation and of public health in the technical sense. Then there was the provision, by charitable benefactors, of special institutions for the sick and the infirm, which grew into the hospital services, first voluntary and then public. There was the prevention of overwork by children and women, out of which there developed our present comprehensive regulations for safeguarding the health of workers in general. There was private medical treatment, beginning with the barber-surgeon of the Middle Ages, and leading on to the employment of thousands of private doctors in the State health insurance scheme. There was the recognition that children could not be expected to profit by education if they were undernourished or underclad or being poisoned by bad teeth or bad tonsils, and that underfed and chronically unwell mothers could not be expected to produce a healthy new generation. This recognition led to the school medical service and to the various arrangements for free or cheap meals and milk, and is now pointing the way to the development of subsidized consumption on a large scale to make sure of a universal minimum of healthy diet. And finally, there was the alarming experience of the last war, when the wholesale rejection of recruits for the army led to the cry that we were a C3 nation; this, and the still more recent realization of how widespread are mental disease and chronic mental ill-health and distortion, have begun to make us aim our health services at prevention rather than cure, and at positive well-being rather than the mere avoidance of actual illness.

Meanwhile, as so often happens in a democracy, new voluntary bodies have been feeling their way into the gaps. Some of these were institutions for treating mental ill-health (as opposed to insanity), such as the Institute of Medical Psychology, with its Tavistock Clinic in Bloomsbury.

In some ways even more significant were organizations like the Peckham Health Centre. This was established to serve a definite area in a typical South London suburb, and on a family basis. Only families, not individuals, could enrol, and only families from Peckham. The preventive aspect was very much to the fore, in the insistence on periodic overhauls of a very thorough nature, so that symptoms could be detected early, and taken in time to prevent real illness. More than that, however, positive well-being was the central aim. Not only did the Centre provide opportunities for physical and mental recreation, but, as well as definite medical treatments and regimes, it also prescribed hobbies and outside interests as what we may call psychological preventive medicine, in the belief that genuine mental interest is a necessity for all-round health.

Other features of the last few years have been the establishment of voluntary health insurance schemes for middle-class people; and the growth (though much less in this country than in the U.S.A.) of specialist teams who between them make a really thorough overhaul of patients, in place of the crop of individual and isolated specialists in Harley Street.

Now let us look at the matter from another angle —the defects of the system as it exists today, and some of the trends that are counteracting the defects. In the first place, the National Health Insurance scheme, with its system of panel doctors, though it has achieved a great deal, still suffers from being conceived in purely curative terms. Its detractors have sometimes said that it is just a gigantic system for indulging the public's taste for bright-coloured and nasty-tasting medicines. While this is a little unfair, it is true that, by and large, the system has not reduced the total amount of sickness in the country, but merely treated it better and made it more bearable. Somehow or other the main emphasis must be laid on the prevention of illness, and on positive health. It should also be remembered that only the insured workers themselves, and not their dependants, are eligible for medical benefit under the health insurance scheme.

Another defect is the class cleavage in our medical service. In general, the better-off consult their private doctors and specialists, and are treated in nursing-homes, while the poorer sections of the community, when they are not consulting their panel doctors, go for advice to some outpatient department, and are treated in the wards of a big hospital. Here again, counteracting tendencies are showing themselves. One is the growth of private health insurance schemes; another is the increasing provision of private wards and rooms for paying patients at big hospitals. But as things are at present, the growth in efficiency of the public hospitals and the public health system in general is being delayed by the snobbery which prefers private treatment at all costs, even in a dingy and expensive private nursing-home, to going into a public institution.

Still a third defect is the existence, side by side, of two quite separate hospital systems—one supported by voluntary organizations, the other maintained by public authorities. The public hospitals have been increasing at a rapid rate, as well as improving in standard, and since 1929 have largely outgrown their old association with charity and the Poor Law. Even before the war, attempts were being made to co-ordinate the two sets of hospitals, as in the Oxford area, where a Joint Hospital Board had already been set up to cover all medical institutions in the region.

The war has brought various important changes, almost all of them tending to counteract one or other of the defects in the system. Thus the State has organized an Emergency Hospital Service, which has provided no fewer than a quarter of a million new hospital beds, over 40,000 of them in new public institutions. These were originally earmarked for the mass casualties which, at the outbreak of war, it was anticipated would be caused by air-raids. However, these have never materialized, and, after a great part of the country's hospital accommodation had lain unused for months, many of the beds have now been turned over for the use of evacuees and other urgent purposes.

National war schemes like that for blood-transfusion have meant more co-operation between different kinds of hospitals, and considerable steps have been taken to regionalize the hospital services and to co-ordinate the different types of institution in each region, rather along the lines already carried out in the Oxford area before the war.

This unification, together with the dispersal of specialists over the country as a whole, has had an interesting effect—it has led to a marked raising of standards in many places. A Harley Street specialist finds himself attached to what was originally, perhaps, a Poor Law hospital in the depths of the provinces, and discovers that this has been jogging along in an old-fashioned routine, cut off from the growing-points of medical science. Naturally, he makes it his business to see that this state of affairs does not continue, and that the latest and most up-to-date methods are introduced. One result has been that many chronic cases among elderly invalids under the Poor Law medical service have had their complaints properly diagnosed for the first time!

Then the danger of epidemics in air-raid shelters has led to the appointment of medical men for all large shelters, together with posts for first-aid and emergency treatment. This is already the rather sketchy embryo of a public system of preventive medicine; but a more radical step towards its development has been taken in certain of the coastal areas that have been partly evacuated for defence reasons. Here an Emergency Medical Service has been set up, operating under the Ministry of Health, and this is already a truly positive health service, with all the doctors and all the institutions of the region unified in a single system under State supervision.

And then there is the new insistence on healthy diet, which I have already spoken of.

The trend would seem fairly clear. It is towards the improvement of environmental agencies of health, such as housing and open spaces, and of that basis of all positive fitness, a really adequate diet; towards the incorporation of more and more doctors, whole or part-time, in a public medical service; an increased emphasis on prevention; the abolishing of the purely private nursing home; then, the extension of the insurance principle to higher income groups, and the giving of more facilities for paying patients at hospitals; next, on co-ordinating more of the different elements in a single unified (but not necessarily uniform) system—both kinds of hospitals, general practitioners and specialists; some arrangement by which specialists pool their knowledge and make it more generally available at lower fees; and finally, the growth of more centres for the encouragement of positive health.

How long it will take to effect this transformation it is impossible to say. To do so will demand a rather radical change of attitude on the part of the medical profession at large, and also of the Ministry of Health. But the change is beginning. The British Medical Association has already set up a strong committee to consider the possible re-organization of the profession; and the Ministry of Health is being forced by the urgencies of air-raid shelters and evacuation to adopt a much more positive policy.

There has never yet been a healthy nation in all the world's history. At last the discoveries of science have given us the possibility of creating one. Our democratic ideals should provide the spur towards translating that possibility into actuality.

VII

The Democratization of Education

WE HAVE just been discussing the past history and present trends of the medical and health services in Britain; now it is the turn of education. Here the situation is in many ways curiously similar. There is the same mixture of voluntary and public institutions, the same class cleavage, though in a more acute form, the same incipient tendency towards unification.

In an earlier chapter I said something about the two systems of education that exist side by side in Britain, one for the rich, the other for the poor, and almost entirely separate until the University stage is reached. Curiously enough, the so-called Public Schools, which are the central core of the rich man's private system, originated in the late Middle Ages and early Renaissance as foundations reserved for poor scholars. Eton, for instance, was originally a college of seventy poor scholars only. The main part of the school, which in 1939 numbered over 1100, consists of fee-paying boys who have clustered round the education provided by the benefaction of King Henry VI. The public schools are typically boarding-schools, and stress tradition, esprit de corps, and character-building. They grade off into certain types of grammar schools and purely private schools, but none of them is State-aided or State-controlled, and they preserve a certain unity through their Headmasters' Conference.

In the eighteenth century, the education of poor children was provided, largely under the influence of religious bodies, by free Charity Schools and the semi-charitable Common Schools, but it was poor in quality and not very extensive in quantity. In the early nineteenth century, the rapid growth of an ignorant proletariat in the cities roused the nation's voluntary effort. But the effort was divided by the religious issue; on one side was a powerful society bent on educating the poor under Church of England auspices, on the other an equally powerful body, backed by nonconformists and free-thinkers, equally determined to keep education out of the hands of the Established Church. Behind both was the economic necessity of providing a modicum of education to children destined to become factory workers or clerks.

By 1833, the Government was brought in to help, but confined its assistance to grants for buildings. The next important step was taken in 1839 when the State first assumed some of the responsibility for training teachers. In 1858, the system of 'payment by results' was introduced, by which grants were made out of the rates (what in America are called local or city taxes) in proportion to the number of children who passed an examination in the three R's.

THE DEMOCRATIZATION OF EDUCATION

But population continued to grow, and popular ignorance continued to be both a scandal and a source of industrial weakness. By 1870, the Government was forced to take the leading role, and established through the agency of locally elected boards what became known as Board Schools, financed out of public funds, to fill the gaps in the voluntary system. Ten years later, elementary education was made compulsory; and within a further ten years all fees for elementary education were abolished. But within the general system the Church schools still persisted side by side with the undenominational State schools.

What I have been saying applies to England. In Scotland, the tradition of public responsibility for education is much older. Many Scottish towns had their own municipal schools and academies as far back as the sixteenth century, and parish schools were provided out of local taxation by the beginning of the seventeen-hundreds. There was also a much greater general feeling for education, and the time-table of the Scottish Universities was arranged so as to make it possible for poor farmers' and crofters' sons to work on the farms during the summer and attend college in the winter. In this, the system was more like that in the United States, where so many young people work their way through College.

Scotland has thus enjoyed three centuries of democratic education, and over a long period the intellectual level attainable, and attained, by the common man was higher than in any other country.

The chief trend of the last fifty years in the English public educational system has been the steady raising of the school-leaving age, and the building up of a public system of secondary education—State-supported secondary schools, State-aided grammar schools, and technical schools. Another important step has been the founding of the School Medical Service, and the provision of cheap or free meals and milk, which I mentioned earlier.

Of late years, quite a number of new public schools have been founded. It must not be forgotten that there exist a great many purely private schools, some of them preparatory to the public schools, but some competing with them; they are not in any way under State control.

The major defect of the system is its class cleavage; broadly speaking, there has been one education for the governing class and the privileged, another for the governed and the under-privileged. Public school boys enjoy certain social advantages, and often find it easier to get a good start in business or a profession, while State-aided education has on the whole been designed to provide training for subordinate positions.

However, the majority of those who are going to occupy key posts in Government, in business, and in the professions are ex-public school boys, and so strong is the realization that the public schools are a

THE DEMOCRATIZATION OF EDUCATION

main bulwark of the British class system, that it has crystallized in the phrase 'the old school tie,' to denote whatever admixture of snobbery and privilege is still to be found in British society.

It should be emphasized that the class cleavage is only serious in southern England. In the north of England, in Scotland, and in Wales, there are few public schools, and a much smaller proportion of the older boys from well-to-do homes are sent to public schools, either locally or in the South. The conditions, in fact, are much more like those in the U.S.A. or in Canada, though at lower ages the children from richer families are almost all sent to private 'prep. schools.'

During the present century considerable progress has been achieved towards making the educational ladder a reality. The extent and quality of public secondary education has been astonishingly improved, and the Universities have been to a large extent democratized through a liberal provision of scholarships.

But the progress has not been so great as it would have been, for various reasons. One is the competition of the public schools, and the mingled snobbery and legitimate ambition which drives so many parents, in spite of the great financial sacrifices required, to send a boy to one of them rather than to a secondary school. Another is the class bias in the State-aided schools as a whole, the conception of them as preparing boys and girls for certain not so desirable careers, instead of developing them in an all-round way as citizens of a progressive and democratic nation. And the educational ladder is very far from complete. A recent careful study has shown that whereas practically every able child in the upper economic classes receives a secondary education, that is true for less than a quarter of the much more numerous children of the manual workers, and for less than a third of those in the intermediate class. Quite apart from the individual frustration involved, the nation is indulging in a scandalous waste of its most precious asset—brain-power.

Meanwhile a quite separate but very important movement for Adult Education had been taking shape. The early nineteenth century saw the foundation of various institutions, such as the Mechanics' Institutes, for what it was then the fashion to call 'the improvement of the working classes.' But in its modern form the movement can be said to date from the establishment of the University Extension system by Cambridge in 1873. Still later, in 1903, the Workers' Educational Association was founded, which works by means of organized classes, and this reaches a high proportion of the studiously inclined among the young workers. However, there is as yet nothing to compare with the Folk High Schools of Denmark, for instance, nothing which can be said to exert an important influence on national life as a whole.

Meanwhile the war is bringing all sorts of new

changes. In the first place, high taxation is making it increasingly difficult for parents to afford a public school education for their boys, and many public schools are already faced with serious financial difficulties. Then there is a great demand for some form of satisfying activity for working boys (and girls too) after they leave school at 14 or 15. There are organized youth movements; there are specialized schemes of pre-military training, like the Air Cadet Corps; there are movements for training the will and the character through the body, like the County Badge movement; there are Youth Service Corps springing up in response to war needs.

With the existence of a huge conscript army, for the most part quartered at home and not yet called on for active service, the need for Army Education has been obvious, and it has grown rapidly. There is room for plenty of improvement in Army Education, especially on the political side, but at least it is already providing adult education on quite a new scale.

The establishment of a separate Polish School of Medicine at Edinburgh is perhaps a step towards the re-establishment of the truly international universities of the Middle Ages.

Another interesting development has been what we may call Air-Raid Education—the provision of lectures and classes in air-raid shelters. In London alone, over 400 classes are being held regularly in public shelters. In addition, large numbers of libraries are being provided in shelters. One man of 65 recently remarked to a shelter librarian, 'I never seemed to have the time to read before this.' The long black-out evenings have stimulated reading in the home as well.

In education, as a whole, it is fairly clear how the trends are moving. I think it is almost certain that within a very few years from the end of the war we shall see, first, the raising of the school-leaving age to 16. Secondly, the provision of a scheme by which some sort of part-time education, not of the formal sort, and involving the body as much as the mind and service as much as instruction, will be universally provided up to 18 or 19, so that adolescence will be given the self-respect and satisfaction that comes through a healthy body, creative activity, and a sense of being useful. Thirdly, the widening of the basis of adult education, so that a really large section of the people, and not merely the small studious minority, take advantage of the opportunities provided: that is a necessary preliminary to the development of a live and self-conscious society. Fourthly, permanent provision will be made for large-scale exchange of children between town and country. Then we shall see the school enlarged and elaborated to play the role of a community centre and not merely a series of classrooms, as has already been done in the Village Colleges in Cambridgeshire and elsewhere. Next, the purely private schools will be abolished, or, if not abolished, altered in character by being put under public control. Then the public schools will in some way or another be brought into a unified national system. The most obvious way would be, as grants of public money become necessary to keep them alive, to make the grants conditional on throwing open, say, a third of the places to selected children from elementary schools, who will then profit by the public schools' tradition and atmosphere. Eventually, we can be pretty sure that they will be turned into special institutions reserved for the young élite of the nation, irrespective of any advantages of birth or wealth. And finally, in this last and in other ways, the reserves of brain-power and talent in the poorer strata of society will be more fully tapped, and made available to their possessors and to the nation at large. The number of free places and scholarships will be increased, and the cost of higher education decreased.

One of the boasts of the British system is its extraordinary variety. Not only is there great variety in the type of the secondary institutions that are now wholly or partly outside public control, but all schools under public control are given the fullest latitude and initiative. Indeed, every headmaster works out his own curriculum—an astonishing contrast to the centralized uniformity of a system like the French.

It is certain, I think, that this variety will be continued; but also clear that the system is bound to become more democratic, both through the breaking down of class barriers between different types of schooling, and through a greater equality of opportunity to profit by higher education; and clear again that the Government will have to play a more active and positive role in the whole business.

I would also hazard the guess that education will be given more of a direction. In earlier centuries, all education had a religious direction. The nineteenth century, in rebellion against the dominance of the Church and the Church's adherence to outworn ideas and reactionary institutions, made all State education strictly secular. In so doing, however, it tended to make it morally neutral and socially colourless. At the same time the tradition persisted of giving the governing classes a classical education, divorced from contact with everyday affairs, and of regarding technical education as something purely utilitarian and rather inferior. The result, even after modern history, modern languages and natural science had found their way into the curriculum, was to lay much too great a stress on the academic and deliberately non-useful and non-practical aspects of education.

If the basic trend within democracy is towards a really organic society, this must be reflected in the educational system. Education will be thought of as a preparation for the business of living together in a particular society, not as a means of acquiring miscellaneous information, or only of fitting yourself for a specific job. You in America are already waking up to this. The retiring vice-president of the Education Section of the American Association for the Advancement of Science has just been reported as saying: 'There are among us people of great influence who really believe that Democracy *can* never be highly efficient. These attitudes of our own citizens are one of the great dangers that American democracy is facing today. It is against these that we must organize and plan education for the defence of democracy.' It would need several chapters to amplify this properly: I must content myself here by saying that education, having escaped from religious direction and classical bias only to become directionless, will acquire a new slant in the shape of a social direction, and correlated with this will be a change in the status of the whole educational system. From being a Cinderella among the social services, it will become central and vital, the projection of the community's ideals into the coming generation that will have to implement them.

The tendencies within these two social services of health and education are to be seen in the others also—to universalize a minimum standard of benefit; to preserve variety; to break down class barriers; and to give exceptional talent the best possible opportunity. As we bring these changes about, democracy (which is still young) will be entering a new stage.

VIII

Planning and Democracy

SO FAR, in our quest for principles to guide a nation which is trying to combine democracy with positive social service, we have reached the following guiding lines. First, we should adopt the principle of standards in different departments of life, and the State should make it its business to see that none of its citizens is deprived of the opportunity of reaching those standards through no fault of his own. Where possible, the standards should be external, scientific and fixed, as in those for health; elsewhere, as with education, they will be arbitrary, and can change and become higher as society progresses, but here too they can be and should be definite, so that the degree by which we fall short of reaching them can be measured.

Then we saw that it was desirable to unify the collection of separate standards by proclaiming a People's Minimum, which should include every aspect of the good life in which the State felt it should and could ensure a reasonable minimum standard to all. It is no good fixing standards too high to start with—saying that everyone shall have a car, or a higher education, or a month's holiday with pay every year: it will be impossible in practice to get anywhere near your standard, and the whole principle will fall into disrepute. But if you begin with a reasonable minimum, this can be raised steadily as time goes on.

And our third general idea was one of method—namely, that for many purposes, notably health and economic security, the family, not the individual, must be the unit.

But there are other general principles that will help us. The one that I shall begin with is the principle of planning. Careful planning becomes a necessity as soon as you begin to realize that *laisser-faire* is not enough; and it becomes necessary on a scale we have hardly begun to envisage once you deliberately throw *laisser-faire* and economic man into the discard, and set about building a truly organized, living community.

Now planning, like positive social service, is a necessity in all modern technological countries, dictatorships as much as democracies. But the problem for the democracies is how to combine efficient planning with democratic freedom and initiative. This is difficult enough; but many people make it out more difficult than it really is. Every time I have been in the United States in recent years some prominent business man or financier was sure to make the headlines with an utterance about planning being the thin end of the totalitarian wedge, about the impossibility of stopping, once you had started any planning, until you had 100 per cent. planning, about the New Deal's planning being a step towards dictatorship, and so on. Mr. Joseph Kennedy was reported on his return to the U.S.A. to have said that democracy in Britain was dead. He later denied having said this; but I expect he thought it, as he most certainly belongs to that large class who think that the essence of democracy is the freedom of individuals to make big fortunes out of big business; and he must have genuinely thought that Britain's controlled war-time economy was the reverse of what he meant by democracy. The need for organizing and speeding up armaments production in the United States has already helped many Americans to change their minds about the necessity of planning in time of war or near-war. But a great many seem to be yearning for a return to individualism, rugged or otherwise, once peace comes.

However, individualism seems only to work satisfactorily in a rapidly expanding system—like the early industrial revolution in Britain, or in America so long as there was a frontier, and open spaces into which to spread. Then I suppose that very few thoughtful persons seriously believe that we in this country will or can go back to an unplanned economy after the war. Certainly most people agree that the continuation of some pretty thoroughgoing control will be necessary for some time after the war, since it is clear that the period of reconstruction will demand what will be in effect a war economy, only without the fighting. Actually, it would seem that the one thing that is impossible is to have half-and-half planning. Planning then gets deadlocked with individualism. You can have quarter-planning, with planning confined to the sectors where individualism is obviously not working. Or you can have three-quarter planning, with a residue of individual initiative supported, economically speaking, on the back of a planned general structure; something like this is likely to be the condition of the post-war world. But the intermediate proportions are not really workable.

The fact that de-control on any large scale after the war would mean chaos for us, is another reason for getting America interested in planning; for unless our two countries agree on a common plan for after the war, God help us and the rest of the world. But even if they agree on the necessity for planning, my original problem remains—how to have efficient planning without sacrificing a great deal of democracy.

There are various ways of keeping democracy vigorous in a planned society. In the first place, most of those who have studied the question think it essential to leave a biggish unplanned sector in peacetime national life. There is no reason why many specialized and luxury trades and businesses should be planned: initiative and variety are needed in them, and in launching certain kinds of new inventions (indeed planning in the field of new inventions is likely to be largely concerned with preventing established competitors from buying them up and suppressing them!). Then to try to plan the really creative activities of man, like pure scientific research, or art, is disastrous, as has been made very plain in Germany. What *can* be done is to plan to provide opportunities for free creative minds: but that is another matter. Nor can discussion and criticism be planned: here again, freedom is of their essence if they are to have any value. Indeed, paradoxical though it may seem at first sight, planning itself should be partly outside the national plan. By that I mean that unofficial and voluntary bodies, like our Institute of International Affairs and in the United States the Institute of Pacific Relations in politics, like our National Institute of Social and Economic Research or in America the National Planning Association in economic and social affairs, are essential parts of a planned democracy. There are safeguards against bureaucratic rigidity in planning, both through their criticisms of official plans, and also through their putting forward alternative plans of their own, or plans that are bolder and more far-reaching than what officialdom can venture on.

Still more important, it is perfectly possible to combine central planning with plenty of local initiative, to bring voluntary effort and voluntary organizations into a planned system, and to grant a great deal of freedom to private firms and institutions within the broad outline of a Government plan. And finally, the undoubted dangers of trying to apply a rigid and uniform plan to a nation which is not uniform but shows strong local differences of attitude and interest, can be countered by adopting the principle of regional planning, in which the most comprehensive planning is done separately for the various separate regions of the country, and the national plan is no more than a general framework, loosely co-ordinating the different regional plans.

I will give a few examples to show what I am driving at. The first is from America—the Tennessee Valley Authority, T.V.A. for short. It illustrates both regional planning and the possibility of keeping local initiative under a plan. I am leaving out of account that aspect of the T.V.A. which, rather unfortunately, got most of the limelight in its early years: I mean the electric power aspect, and the use of the T.V.A. as a yardstick for the price and supply of electricity by private Utility Companies. The really important fact about the T.V.A. is that it is the biggest and best experiment in general planning in any democratic country. I went all over it a few years ago, so that I can speak with some first-hand knowledge.

At headquarters, the T.V.A. has a comprehensive plan for the huge region over whose destinies it has been put in control. This plan has been worked out on thoroughly scientific lines, and takes in agriculture; the conservation of soil, of water-power, of mineral wealth, of game, and of forests; health, diet, housing (the standards of which were in general very low in the region); education, development of farming and of rural industries by means of cheap power, amenities and the tourist industry, and so on.

But the working out of the plan is not entrusted to an army of T.V.A. employees. Wherever possible, the T.V.A. works through existing organizations. Its area comprises parts of several separate States, and we all know how jealous States are of their rights; within each State there are cities, each with its own administration, and all the machinery of local government by county and so on. To put the matter as simply as possible, the T.V.A. works by getting the local authorities to work for it. And it gets the local authorities to work for it by advice combined with grants. The advice is expert advice, good advice, so that men of goodwill and sense will generally want to follow it. If they do not happen to like it, whether on political grounds or because they are not ready to appreciate its value, or for whatever other reason, then money begins to talk: grants will be available for schemes that fit in with the general plan, but not for those that run counter to it, and certainly not for masterly inactivity. Advice and grants together have seen to it that the broad lines of the plan are being realized, and, what is more, with the active co-operation and often enthusiasm of the local people.

Sometimes these suggest the modification of a scheme to suit local needs, and if this fits in with the general plan, it will be accepted. In any case, the execution is left largely in their hands, and they have the inspiring sense of being active partners in a big creative enterprise.

The T.V.A. ropes in private enterprise as well as local authorities to help in this way. For instance, when they want to demonstrate some new agricultural method, they do not use a public demonstration farm, but get a private farmer to volunteer to use it. If he succeeds, this carries much more conviction with other farmers, as well as making him keener himself.

Of course there are certain fields in which the T.V.A. itself has to execute as well as plan—the broad lines of power policy; where the dams and storage reservoirs are to be located, when and how they are to be built; forest and game conservation; and so on. But in most fields there is plenty of scope left for local initiative and freedom within the plan.

Another important point about the T.V.A. is its regional character. It operates in a region big enough to make large-scale planning worth while in matters like flood-control or electric power; but not too big to include fundamentally different problems of life and interests. The Tennessee Valley is, from the standpoint of human biology today, a natural region, and one of the right order of size for planning.

Another example of freedom within a planned system comes from English public education. Elementary education is compulsory between the ages of 5 to 15, and certain standards must be attained. But there is the greatest latitude as regards the details of the work; indeed, every headmaster is free to work out his own curriculum, though, of course, the examination system sets a limiting framework. Then there is also freedom in the shape of alternatives to suit different types of mind. At 11, the cleverest children have the chance of qualifying for a secondary school, while others above the average are selected for central schools, where they stay till 15, and where the curriculum is something like that of the early stages of a secondary school. A further alternative is provided at 13, when selected children are sorted out into technical, commercial, art, and domestic science schools.

Or take another example, from physical planning. When the centre of Coventry was recently destroyed by German bombs, the city architect was ready with a plan for a new civic centre for the town. The Ministry of Works and Buildings, which had been made responsible for the physical reconstruction of the country as a whole, agreed that a reconstructed Coventry fitted into its general plan; they approved the detailed scheme, and so the city will get a reconstructed centre designed by its own officials on their own initiative.

PLANNING AND DEMOCRACY

Physical planning illustrates admirably the urgent need for Government to take the initiative in positive service. Planning under our present Town and Country Planning Act is essentially permissive and negative. It permits local authorities to plan, and it lays down a great many rules about what is not allowed. But it is not positive; it does not insist on plans being executed, and it has no general plan for the country as a whole. Again, it permits the purchase of land on either side of arterial roads, to prevent ribbon development. But it did not compel the power to be used; and ribbon development has, with a few exceptions, continued.

As there was no over-riding central plan for the location of industry, some regions, like London, went on growing until they were much too big, while others, like the depressed areas, were forced ever deeper into distress. As each local authority was its own master, and jealous of interference, it proved virtually impossible to make plans for national parks in areas involving several local authorities, such as the Lake District. As different Government departments and statutory bodies acted independently, without central guidance, the Forestry Commission, for instance, might and did cover with ugly conifers areas of mountain and moor that should have been preserved for their natural beauty; or the War Office could sterilize a coastal area that should have been kept for recreation by dumping down a tank training station.

Vested interests in building and land led to large stretches of the countryside being half-suburbanized and spoilt in the most haphazard way. Speculation in site values has prevented the proper replanning of towns and the speeding up of city traffic. The recent setting up of a special committee to prevent this sort of speculation in bombed areas is a recognition that this lesson has at last been learnt.

In all this, it was not radical planning which interfered with freedom; it was *laisser-faire* and private interests, and it was half-hearted planning. Freedom to enjoy wild nature; freedom of easy access to an unspoilt countryside; freedom to live a full and pleasant life in cities, instead of spending long hours every day in uncomfortable travel, returning after work to mere dormitory suburbs—these freedoms can only be enjoyed, in any modern industrial country, under bold and comprehensive planning.

Local government also provides plenty of outlets for individual freedom and initiative within a general plan. Every English county, for instance, is responsible for most of the details of education within its boundaries. Every city can have its own town-planning scheme. Every borough can find work for its public-spirited men and women on all kinds of committees. The staff of every college and university can act as a centre of enlightenment for its own region. In a word, far from planning spelling the end of freedom, we are now beginning to realize that in the rapidly filling-up world of modern industrial society, unplanned *laisser-faire* destroys more freedoms than it keeps alive. Planning, in modern conditions, is becoming an urgent necessity for the retention of what is after all decent human life, unharassed by constant insecurity or needless physical and mental discomfort, and provided with opportunities for self-development. One can, in fact, plan for freedom as well as for efficiency.

We have seen that to ensure the minimum standard of individual well-being, the State must step in as an active, positive instrument of social service. This is itself planning; and a properly planned minimum of security and well-being at once releases a great flow of social energies that otherwise get taken up in constant worry over the mechanical business of existence. Just the same is true of order. Neither voluntary effort nor competing private interests are able to remove the ugliness and disorder that are cluttering up our lives; the State must step in as an active planning agent to ensure order and to preserve and create beauty in our collective existence.

IX

The Development of Backward Areas

WE HAVE laid down three principles of which a democratic social service State must take account of if its policy was to be active and positive, and not merely one of regulatory tinkerings. One is a national minimum for its citizens; a second is comprehensive planning; and the last is development of backward areas. I have tried to deal, however briefly and imperfectly, with the first two; now we come to the third. It is of course obvious that in many ways the three hang together. It is impossible to secure your national minimum without doing a good deal of large-scale and careful planning; and a comprehensive plan will clearly have to take special account of the weak spots in the whole—the depressed areas and backward regions. None the less, this last principle deserves separate consideration. Today I want to talk about the development of backward areas as part of the job of British democracy outside its own country. This is a novel idea to many people. The principle is briefly this—that it will pay in the long run to spend a great deal in getting rid of backward conditions. A region cannot play a satisfactory role in world affairs, whether in producing or consuming goods or in cultural ways, or in making contributions to

THE DEVELOPMENT OF BACKWARD AREAS

culture or scientific knowledge or international understanding, until it is properly equipped to do so. If a firm wants to start production of motor-cars, say, or textiles, it has first of all to incur a considerable outlay on sites, buildings, machinery, skill and brains. This is the capital equipment of the business. In the same way, but on a much more comprehensive scale, a backward area needs capital equipment before it can be expected to function properly as part of the world's economic life. It must have roads, railways, harbours, storage and marketing facilities, power; its rivers must be tamed, its forests properly exploited, its soil conserved and drained and fertilized, its dangerous diseases brought under control; its people must be equipped with a reasonable standard of health and security and education.

What is more, this principle is of special concern to this country, because Britain is the greatest colonial power, which means that it is responsible for more of the world's backward areas than any other nation.

Now backward areas inside your own country are one thing, but backward colonies far off in the tropics and inhabited by people of another colour and culture have a way of looking quite different. In point of fact, the principle of developing backward areas played no part at all in the ideas of colonial powers in earlier periods. On the contrary, direct exploitation in one form or another was the earliest motive. Precious metals, rare products like spices, a supply of slaves, one-sided trade bargains —those are what the colonizers aimed at in the first stages of colonization. Later, when crude exploitation of this sort was no longer possible, the indirect method of exploitation that economic historians call mercantilism became the dominant principle. The dependent country was on no account to be allowed to produce anything that might compete with home industries. Its primary function was to produce any raw materials the metropolitan country might need, and to serve as an outlet for its manufactured products and its younger sons; the system of taxation and tariffs and of trade in general was designed to produce a flow of wealth from the colony to the mother country.

This was the system under which Ireland was ruled for centuries, and the system which lost Britain her North American colonies and gave the world the U.S.A.

This principle is still far from dead. Quite recently, for instance, sanction was refused for the setting-up of a bag factory in Kenya to utilize locally-grown sisal fibre, on the ground that this would compete with industries in Britain; and Britain's economic policy in Palestine has been vitiated in this way. However, the mercantilist principle has in recent times been modified by further ideas. One is the idea of using colonies to settle large numbers of citizens from the home country—as practised by Italy in North Africa, and as advocated by influential sections in this country, and even more in the Union of South Africa, for the East African highlands. Another is concerned with power politics, and sees colonies as reservoirs of man-power for armies; this has been the policy in many French colonies. And the original mercantilist idea has often been coloured by nationalist aims of self-sufficiency. Here again French tropical Africa, with its trade virtually tied to that of France by tariffs and subsidies, was a case in point; and this is one of the main motives behind the Nazis' claim for colonies.

It is only quite recently that economists have begun to think in the all-round long-range way which leads to our principle of development. Once they did so, it became clear that development would pay. It will pay, but only in a comprehensive way, when you think of production and trade as a whole, and not of any particular source of present revenue or the profits of any particular firm; and only in a long-term way, for it may take years or even generations before profits begin to come in, and many of the returns will not be assessable in purely economic terms. Unaided private enterprise cannot be expected to invest in such comprehensive development, with returns so indirect and so long delayed; so here too the State must step in if the principle is to be put into practice.

Perhaps the whole matter becomes clearer when

viewed the other way round. With the world as interdependent as it has grown, a backward region is bound to be a drag on the rest of the world, chiefly because it is so undeveloped as a market. And the more thoroughly world economy is planned and controlled, the more obvious will be the drag thus imposed.

One word of warning. The principle holds good only for areas with adequate natural resources. There are some regions so barren, and others that have been developed so wastefully or in such wrong directions, that they have to come on the world's poor relief, so to speak. But these are very much in the minority.

Now let me get down to some concrete illustrations. As examples of backward regions inside a modern industrial nation let me take large parts of the Old South in the U.S.A., and the depressed areas in Britain. The Old South is potentially rich; but for various reasons it has lagged behind in development. Its backwardness can therefore be cured by providing the capital equipment needed to develop it. This is being done in some parts through the starting of new industries by private initiative, and in the Tennessee Valley by the comprehensive plans of the T.V.A., of which I spoke in an earlier chapter. There can be little doubt that, by itself, the method of private initiative will only work in a few favoured localities, but that once the T.V.A. has built a general foundation, private initiative will be helped instead of hindered throughout the region. I would venture to prophesy that within a generation the major part of the backward South will be in process of development by a number of regional planning agencies.

The British depressed areas are rather different. They have not always been backward: they have become backward because prosperity has departed from them. Their mineral resources have been exhausted: or they have concentrated too much on a single type of industry; or the changing currents of trade have left them high and dry. In any case, their backwardness is not that of under-development but of decay.

Here a good deal can undoubtedly be done by wise spending on the development of new types of industry, but measures must also be taken to transfer industry elsewhere. This can only be done in relation to a general plan for the whole country; and such a plan must allow for the large-scale transfer of population to new and planned communities.

But, as I said before, the core of this problem lies elsewhere, in the under-developed tropical colonies.

The tropical colonies are the most backward part of the globe, with the possible exception of parts of the Arctic regions. If you happened to be a negro baby born in one of the less developed parts of tropical Africa, you would have only a one-in-three or even a one-in-two chance of surviving the first year of life. You would be practically certain to suffer from some dietary deficiency, from some chronic infection such as malaria, and from gross parasites such as round-worms and hookworms. You would be lucky if you received any education at all; in most parts of Central Africa perhaps three-quarters of the children never see a school. Even if you were one of the lucky ones, you would be unlikely to get more than the three R's and the catechism, or at best a simple elementary schooling. Thus you would probably grow up illiterate, in a preponderatingly illiterate community.

You would be most likely to live in a windowless hut, cultivating the soil in a primitive way, paying your taxes either by growing some staple crop for sale, or by travelling on foot long distances to work for extremely low wages in a mine or on a plantation. You would much more likely than not be a good hundred miles from the nearest railway and might well have never seen a metalled road.

If the countryside round your village was not virgin tropical forest, it would be likely to be overgrazed and eroded scrubland, or else so infested with tsetse-fly as to make cattle-keeping impossible. Wild beasts, or poisonous snakes, or disease-carrying insects, or all three, would be part of the permanent background of your life.

This is not a satisfactory state of affairs, whether you look at it from the standpoint of the world at large, or of this country, or of the native peoples of Africa. It is no good pretending that you can keep primitive peoples 'unspotted from the world.' The modern world has already invaded Africa, though in a patchy sort of way, with its missionaries, traders, administrators, planters, mines like those of Rhodesia and Katanga, big businesses like the United Africa Company on the West Coast. The tropics are already infected with what we call civilization. Fundamental change has begun, and is bound to continue; the only hope is to try to guide it in the right direction.

I have been in Central Africa, and can vouch for the fact that in general British colonial administration reaches a remarkably high standard of fairness and justice and paternal benevolence. But it must be admitted that a positive policy of development has been largely lacking. The Italians have spent incomparably more on their African colonies than we on ours. The Dutch have undertaken a much more all-round development of their East Indian Empire than we have attempted anywhere.

We have made a beginning with a new and better policy—indeed we did so actually during the war. The Colonial Development Act increases the amount that may be spent each year on developing our tropical colonies from one to five million pounds, lays down that it may be spent on social developments such as education and health instead of only on projects expected to bring in a commercial profit, and allocates an additional half-million for scientific research in and on the colonies and their problems. (This new policy, by the way, was largely the outcome of a notable piece of research—Lord Hailey's monumental African Survey—which was started by private initiative, and carried through under the auspices of a voluntary body, and with the help of American money from one of the great research foundations.)

This is certainly a real step in the right direction. But it is quantitatively so insufficient that it shows that the nature of the problem has not really been grasped. Five million pounds is not of the right order of magnitude. To make a beginning which will guarantee that the backward tropics can take an adequate place in the world's affairs within the next generation or so, fifty millions a year would be nearer the mark. We have to think in terms of numerous large-scale regional development agencies, on the same sort of pattern as the T.V.A., but with relatively larger budgets, since both the physical and the social backwardness of Africa is much greater than that of the Tennessee Valley. In general, colonial governments will have to think more in terms of development, less exclusively in terms of administration.

But development can be along totalitarian lines as well as along democratic ones. So, even if we were to begin developing the world's backward areas on an adequate scale, we should still have to see that the development squares with democratic principles. This does not imply immediate political democracy with its apparatus of votes and elected representatives, but does mean, I take it, that the development must be primarily for the benefit of the native peoples, not primarily for the advantage of the colonial power, or of national or international big business, remote in the capitals of white men's countries.

Furthermore, there must be a political aim side by side with the material aim; and in a democratic setup that political aim can only be a steadily increasing measure of self-government.

Various methods of safeguarding the material interests of the local inhabitants can be thought of. Development can be entrusted to purely official bodies after the pattern of the T.V.A. Or private capital can be attracted to development agencies operating under some form of charter, which regulates conditions of employment, gives government some control of policy, and insists that all profits above a certain minimum must be ploughed back, so to speak, into the further development of the region. Existing private companies can be made to accept similar regulations.

Then the colonies' political future must be safeguarded. Lord Hailey, in his African Survey, has stressed the need for throwing open more posts to the local inhabitants. In some colonies, such as the Gold Coast, Africans already occupy high positions in the Government. But increasing self-government should be made the general basis of colonial policy. An explicit pronouncement is needed, stating that local inhabitants will be eligible to any position, up to the highest, in the administration of their own country, as they become qualified; and that the educational system will be designed to give them the necessary qualifications. Africans are already widely employed as teachers, as clerks, as technical assistants in forestry, medicine, agriculture, and the like; under the system of indirect rule, they already look after a great deal of local government and local justice, though under the benevolent supervision of white administrators. The experience of the Belgian Congo and the African West Coast shows conclusively that the best Africans, given proper education and training and adequate outlets for their abilities, are just as competent as white men, and this is even more obvious with most Asiatics. In a couple of generations, under an enlightened educational and political system, the majority of responsible positions in the colonies—in business, in the professions, in politics, in the higher ranks of the administration—could be occupied by men drawn from the ranks of their own peoples. The essential is that the system shall be gradually built up on a strong foundation of local self-government and that native initiative is given a chance to prove itself first in the innumerable positions of real but minor responsibility that will be available if large-scale development is to become a reality.

And local tradition and local pride must be encouraged if the tropics are to make their contribution to the world's culture.

Development of backward areas on a large scale is necessary for the world's long-term prosperity; and that development must be to an increasing extent self-development if the world system is to be a democratic one.

Meanwhile, however, self-government must still remain a remote goal for most tropical colonies. In the interim, measures must be taken to guard against imperialist exploitation. For numerous reasons, international administration is both impractical and undesirable. But it is desirable to submit national administration to some international supervision. The most urgent need is for uniformity of standard: some colonial powers fall far below others in their administration. The Mandates Commission of the League did useful work, but was not altogether satisfactory. A better method would be to work through a series of International Conventions, after the pattern of those drawn up by the International Labour Office. This would make it possible to raise standards progressively.

For this, of course, some international body will be needed; but what that shall be depends on many imponderables. Whatever form international organization may take, however, it is essential that the central political body shall have a colonial section, with its own research and advisory staff, and a budget for development. Through such a body, the bridge could be built between the national administration and the international supervision of colonies.

X

Democracy between Nations

CAN democratic principles be extended into international affairs? Assuredly. One has only to look at Nazi methods and ideals in this sphere to realize that they are radically undemocratic, while we or the U.S.A. are at least attempting to apply some of the principles of democracy in our dealings with other nations.

On the other hand, it is only too true that international morality lags a long way behind private morality, and that while we have at least some pattern in our mind for the working of democracy within a nation, even this is lacking for any attempt to make democratic ideals work as between nation and nation.

No matter—then we must make up our minds to work out that pattern; for we can be sure that, if democratic principles are essentially sound and right, they will apply between nations just as much as between individuals.

Here Britain has made one fundamental contribution. We have invented a new pattern of international co-operation—the British Commonwealth of Nations. So far as Britain and the Dominions are concerned, this has no elaborate machinery or constitution to hold it together, nothing comparable to the Federal Constitution uniting and overriding the States of the U.S.A. Its only formal focus is the monarchy, which serves as a symbolic centre; its only administrative machinery is the system of Imperial Conferences which discuss its affairs every four years, together with the Governor-Generals and High Commissioners who provide continuous liaison between its parts.

Its unity depends in large measure on the set of common values shared by its members, which in turn ensure that in general they share common interests as well. In addition, there is a material basis. Britain is by far the most powerful member of the group and not only supplies naval and other protection to the rest but also actual armaments: and there are no strings attached. It is for these reasons that the Dominions have joined wholeheartedly with Britain in this and in the last war. There is one exception: Eire has chosen to remain neutral in this war, thus illustrating the absence of compulsion within the Commonwealth system.

The Boer War may have had its bad Imperialist side, but the peace that followed granted independent status to the conquered nation, and eventually allowed and indeed encouraged it to become the dominant partner in the Union of South Africa. The value of freedom in international relations was never better demonstrated. In spite of the past, and in spite of some internal opposition, South

Africa has of its own free will decided to come in with Britain both in this war and the last.

And the system has been partially extended to other nations, such as Egypt. The British treatment of Egypt has also been criticized as Imperialist, and it is clearly in Britain's interests, so long as there is danger of war, to keep some control over Egypt as the key to the East and the vital centre of Empire communications. But the arrangement has worked well by which Egypt, under this modicum of control, enjoys political independence, and Egypt has been a very willing partner in providing a base for British operations in Libya—while at the same time being protected against the aggression that would undoubtedly have been practised against her if she had been wholly outside the British system.

Contrast this state of affairs with the Nazis' treatment of Europe. Hitler's so-called 'New Order' there has to be maintained by huge armies of occupation, and its central idea is one of domination, not of equal partnership. The Germans are the *Herrenvolk*, the chosen rulers, and the rest of Europe must accept the role of subject colonies —and what is more, colonies that are run on mercantilist lines, with all their trade and industry having to adjust itself to the business of supplying Germany with what she needs, in return for the goods she wants to dispose of. On the other hand, Germany is doing something of value. She is converting Europe into a single economic and political unit, even if her method of doing so is an abominable one and cannot last. And by her series of aggressions on small nations—Austria and Czechoslovakia, then Poland, then Norway, Denmark and Holland, and now Rumania and Bulgaria, she has taught the world a bitter but necessary lesson—that the sovereign right of small nations to neutrality can no longer be tolerated. Neutrality is finished as a political concept: it represented, we now realize, merely a series of fatally weak spots in the not overstrong fabric of political security.

The democratic idea of freedom was pushed to extremes in international affairs, under the guise of the doctrine of unrestricted and absolute national sovereignty. But the complementary idea of fraternity was almost absent; apart from the League of Nations, which we realize now was designed on faulty principles, there was no machinery for giving expression to it in the relations of nations with each other. Nations were unwilling either to sacrifice their sovereign rights to a common pool of peace and security, or to make adequate positive contributions to such a pool.

The doctrine of unlimited national sovereignty was the counterpart in international affairs of the extreme doctrine of individualism within society. Once you began to analyse them critically, they turned out to be fictions. The personal freedom of individualism led in practice to the curtailment of freedom for most individuals. In practice, the absolutely sovereign nation was always having to adjust itself to the fact that it existed in a world of other nations, with other interests. Insistence on unrestricted sovereignty, as happened all too tragically with the claim of small nations to remain neutral, led to sovereignty disappearing altogether.

In an essentially similar way, unrestricted sovereignty in the economic sphere led to cut-throat competition, with every nation trying to force as much as possible of its own products on others, and to take as little as possible in return, and to become self-sufficient. In the long run, the resulting tangle of tariffs, quotas, subsidies and exchange restrictions effectually damped down the total volume of world trade so much that more and more people were thrown out of work and general distress increased. The logical outcome was an attempt at autarky or complete self-sufficiency: but this was never really practicable for any single nation, and for Germany the inescapable result of the attempt was war, to secure new sources of supply and new outlets for manufactured exports.

Concerted action is needed between nations just as much as within nations. Between nations it is necessary to create a reasonable minimum of security against war, a reasonable minimum of stability against fluctuations in production and trade, a reasonable minimum of planned order in the world, a reasonable rate of development for backward areas. Somehow, the relations of whole countries must be organized for mutual security and service, just as national government must be organized for social security and service. If we fail in the attempt to do this, we shall deserve the new wars and the more violent disasters that will unquestionably result. The aggressor nations have developed the technique of bullying and intimidation to such a point that country after country has fallen into their grip. The world must build up arsenals of security to counter this exploitation of insecurity.

But there are some hopeful signs. Since September, the U.S.A. has become fully awake to the fact that it is thoroughly entangled in world affairs, whether it likes it or not. It has realized that for the past century or so it, like the small maritime countries of Europe, has been able to enjoy its independence and go peaceably about its business because the British Navy has acted as a general police force as well as an instrument of national power. It has realized that the price of security is planned co-operation.

Some remarkable new measures are the result of this realization. One is the principle of hemispheric defence, with the swapping of destroyers for British bases in the western hemisphere, the thoroughgoing scheme for joint defence between Canada and the U.S.A. and the further joint defence schemes now being worked out in the Pacific.

Another is the revolutionary lease-and-lend principle, by which the supremacy of money and finance and most of the usual formalities of dealings between separate nations have been short-circuited. These are exceedingly practical expressions of our principle that co-operation is the price of security.

The steps already taken open the door to a new and more hopeful system of security. The civilized world needs arsenals of security against barbaric aggression; and the United States and Britain could provide these arsenals. Within a year, the United States should have the biggest arms production of any nation. The armaments they are producing are standardized so that they can be used by us or by them according to the needs of the moment. And when I say *us*, I include also the various contingents from other nations that are fighting with us—the Polish, the Dutch, the Norwegian, the Belgian, the Free French, and of course the Dominions and Indian forces.

When the war is won, the U.S.A. and the British Commonwealth can continue this co-operation for security. Instead of creating economic chaos by closing down armaments factories wholesale, we can continue turning out stocks of the weapons necessary for modern war—planes, tanks, heavy guns, submarines and large warships. That will be our distinctive contribution to the security problem. That of Germany will be a compulsory contribution, the giving up of the right to manufacture arms at all. That of the small nations of Europe will be the sacrifice of their sovereign right to neutrality. They and we will join to form what may be called a Security Club, in which Britain and America, jointly, would play the same kind of role as regards the supply of arms that is played by Britain within the British Commonwealth.

Stocks of these weapons could be accumulated at strategic points in both hemispheres. These would be the arsenals of world security. Other nations which had joined the Security Club would be able to send contingents for training in the use of the special weapons in these arsenals—but not to build up stocks of them in their own countries. Separate nations in peace-time would thus be restricted to armed forces in the nature of a militia, armed only with lighter weapons.

If there were a threat of aggression, whether from some country outside the Anglo-American orbit, or from some European nation which in spite of everything had managed to re-arm, then the necessary armaments could be rushed from the nearest security arsenal to the countries that were threatened, where they could at once be employed by the contingents already trained in their use, together with contingents from other powers as need be. In this way, the great defect of all previous systems of security could be overcome—the absence of physical preparation, and the delay involved, when a peaceable country is attacked, in making good its deficiency in armaments.

Some such realistic approach would be worth more to the cause of democratic security and freedom in international affairs than all the pacts in the world.

The same realistic approach is needed in other fields. Thus in the economic field, it will be better to build up *ad hoc* international bodies for controlling trade or production. They can be made to limit national economic sovereignty in point of actual fact, while attempts to do so by defining the degree of limitation in a paper constitution are likely to remain on paper.

It would take too long to go into details of any such economic schemes. But various experts believe that the creation of international controls for perhaps a dozen key raw materials could be made the foundation-stone of world economic stability and of steady expansion of consumption. The various controls would be under a single Raw Materials Union, which, as with military security, would have to comprise the U.S.A. and the British Empire as its indispensable core, together with such other nations as wanted to join the club, so to speak, and were considered eligible to do so. And further machinery for regulating tariffs and exchanges would of course be necessary, though long-term arrangements for the supply of raw materials would be the sheet anchor of stability.

A properly organized set of raw material controls would provide a simple method of preventing any nation from illegal rearmament—cut off the raw materials, and heavy arms simply cannot be made. Modern air power, too, not only makes it easier to detect any infringement, but is also a valuable aid in stopping it.

Within Europe itself after the war (which I am assuming will be properly won, for there can be no planning for a peaceful future if it is lost or drawn), the situation for some years must obviously be one where Britain continues to play a dominant part, but backed up by the Dominions and the United States. Britain would be the chief European agent for the firm of world democracy. But as conditions improved, some form of European Union must take shape. We should be wise if we took the experience of the British Empire, and built along Commonwealth rather than Federal lines; though clearly there would have to be rather more central machinery than in the British Commonwealth.

And the world would do well to take another leaf out of the British book. As I said earlier, the British Commonwealth does not regulate its affairs by setting up a written constitution, or indeed any fixed system at all, but by a series of Imperial Conferences. These provide the flexibility and the give-and-take which are part of the essence of democratic method.

Would it not be wise to do the same for peace, both European peace and world peace? A single Peace Conference which is expected to lay down the framework of the world for a whole epoch is in modern conditions a virtual impossibility. Why not conferences at regular intervals, say, every two years, at which, in a series of temporary conventions, the new world system could be gradually built up, and by which at the same time the opportunity for peaceful change would be provided?

In discussing this topic I have indulged in much more speculation than in the others. But this was unavoidable, because international morality and international organization is so behindhand. But I hope I have shown that democratic principles can be extended into the international field, and that the only secure basis for so doing will be real agreement and active co-operation between Britain and the United States after the war.

XI

Disintegration and Reintegration

SO FAR, I have said a great deal about what society, through its organs of government, ought to do for its citizens, in providing social services and in planning for stability and for a fuller and more ordered life; but nothing about what the citizens ought to do for the society to which they belong. To employ the usual phrasing, I have discussed rights but not duties. This does not mean that I do not think them important. On the contrary, without a lively sense of duty and a proper system of outlets for it in the shape of service, no community can be truly alive and vigorous. However, as with social services and with planning, so with duty and service. Man's desire to feel useful, to contribute to a greater whole, can be made part of the driving force of a totalitarian state just as readily as of a democratic one. But its expression has to be quite different. In Germany, the method adopted is blind obedience within the framework of the leadership system. No one will deny that it has generated a fanatical spirit of service and indeed of sacrifice, or that it has heightened the national sense of living unity to an extraordinary degree. How can we harness this potent force and yet remain democratic? Somehow we

DISINTEGRATION AND REINTEGRATION

must do so if our societies are to remain vigorous. Indeed it is only by so doing that we can hope to become really democratic; for duties and service are the concrete expression of that fraternity which democracy has as yet hardly begun to realize in practice.

This war is providing outlets in plenty, many of quite new types, for service. There is of course military service; there are the A.R.P. and the Auxiliary Fire-fighting Services; the Women's and other voluntary services; the various Youth Service Corps; and a dozen others. These are definite organizations; in addition, outlets for service are growing up spontaneously in the shape of shelter committees, neighbourhood clubs, and the like.

Let me give one or two concrete examples. In Liverpool, a Liverpool Youth Service Corps has been formed, of boys from 16 to 19. Not every applicant is successful in joining. Once boys have joined, they have to undergo a stiff training before they qualify for their badge. No bribes, in the shape of recreation or special privileges, are offered —merely hard work and a high standard both of attendance and performance. They are warned that the Liverpool Youth Service Corps is harder to get into and easier to be kicked out of than any other service organization; they are told that their business is always to put something in, never to get anything out of the organization.

Yet they do get a great deal out of it. I was talking recently to one of the men chiefly responsible for the organization, and he told me that the results were astonishing. 'The boys are ready to die for Liverpool,' he said: 'and if there are more bad air-raids they will certainly be in the thick of the danger.' Many of them are from the worst slums of the city, and in peace spent a good deal of their spare time dodging the police. Now they have a new pride in themselves—a new cleanliness, a new care for their clothes and appearance, a new look in their eyes. Many others are from well-to-do homes, with a peacetime tradition of merely having a good time in their leisure. Yet both kinds have been given a real devotion to their city. They all feel that they are being of some use in the world. In some jobs, like carrying messages and putting out incendiary bombs, they are actually better than grown men.

There is one instance of an organized outlet for the spirit of devotion, or, if you prefer less exalted language, for the desire to be useful, that lurks in every human being. The Home Guard and the A.R.P. wardens provide plenty of other examples. After a hard day's work, men take pride in turning out for duty night after night, exposing themselves to bombs, digging among debris to rescue buried victims until they are ready to drop with fatigue.

The spirit of service can equally be mobilized to meet a sudden emergency. The best example perhaps was the flotilla of mixed craft, manned by sea-going men of every sort, from rich yachtsmen to bargees, who rescued the Expeditionary Force from the beaches of Dunkirk.

No, there is no question that the spirit of service is there, waiting to be called upon, and that when it does find outlets, it brings new satisfactions to the individual as well as new vigour and unity to the group. Indeed, the words *individual* and *society*, we are coming to realize, are empty abstractions if used by themselves. It is only in the inter-relations between individual and society that both become real and concrete.

However, it is comparatively easy to mobilize the spirit of service in war-time. There is an enemy to defeat, there is tangible damage to be repaired; it is like a game in that there it a definite goal to aim at, tangible manoeuvres of an opposing side to meet and overcome. In peace, there is no single enemy, no single goal; and unity begins to break down. And in general people think of war service and war sacrifice as part of a national emergency; but they quite rightly do not like to think of the state of emergency being prolonged through years of peace.

None the less it is urgent that we should try to think how service shall be organized in peace-time; for without the cement which that provides, society is not likely to cohere. To do this means embarking on a task much more difficult than anything I have yet attempted—the visualizing of a society differing in type and framework from that which now exists. But before attempting this, let me say why I think that this effort is necessary, why it is necessary to look beyond any mere patching and tinkering, towards the transformation of our society into one of new type and nature.

We have got to remember that we are living through one of the revolutionary phases of history, in which a doomed but still active system is struggling with forces and ideas that are destined to bring a new world order to birth. It is not always easy to realize this crucial fact. The fact is too huge, the steps too gradual: it is like trying to estimate the passage of time on a watch with only an hour-hand. Besides, human nature mostly finds the idea of revolutionary change extremely distasteful, and manages to protect itself against the notion that it is living through such a period. Some you hear saying, 'It can't happen here,' while others deny that it is happening at all, or react by defending, with new and desperate vigour, the familiar ideas in which they have grown up.

But it is happening, and it is happening everywhere, though at different rates and in different detailed ways in different countries. Everywhere the old system, of capitalist profit-making and individualist competition, of nationalist rivalry and imperialist expansion, is falling to bits; and in the long run the one really important question is whether a new system can be built up in time to save the world from chaos. Some countries, like Germany, and in an anaemic sort of way, Vichy France, have already suffered revolution. In others, like Spain, there has been revolution and counter-revolution. But for us, who believe in democracy, the new systems brought into being by these upheavals are repugnant, and we hope and believe that they are but temporary crystallizations, temporary reactions against the new advancing forces. For Britain and America, the problem is whether they can pass through the revolutionary period by evolution without suffering the horrors of revolution in the narrow sense, and emerge with a new type of system that shall set the pattern for the world's new phase.

But disintegration is at work, and the more it proceeds on its way, the more reaction it provokes, and the more danger there is of a counter-revolution of fascist or semi-fascist type, aimed at preserving power in the old privileged hands. This would spell the temporary eclipse of democracy. And that danger can only be overcome by a fairly radical transformation of society. The transformation, if it is to be satisfactory, must give expression to the new forces that are stirring in the world, must satisfy humanity's cravings for security and order, for self-realization and service, but also must take place within a democratic frame. It must, in other words, provide a reintegration of our disintegrating democratic society. There is a race on between disintegration and reintegration; and if disintegration gets too big a lead, reaction and counter-revolution will get their chance to substitute their anti-democratic brand of reintegration.

The trouble in any revolutionary phase like the present is that there are so many competing urgencies. Stability and order look very urgent when chaos threatens; many people sincerely prefer them to freedom. Security looks very urgent to those with unemployment hanging over their head in threat or engulfing them in actuality, to those others who have seen all their savings swallowed up by inflation, or their livelihood going down the drain in the great depression; it was this longing for security which brought so many Germans over to Hitler's side, and in our democratic countries it will weigh heavily against freedom if keeping freedom means also keeping economic insecurity. Satisfaction and fulfilment, the possibility of pride in oneself and one's nation, look very urgent to the frustrated. This craving for national self-respect was another powerful motive which rallied Germans to Hitler. And if democracy cannot promise some satisfactory outlet to the multitude of frustrated men and women in our countries, they will throw democracy overboard for whatever solution offers any chance of self-realization and self-respect.

And then there are the entrenched forces of vested interest and privilege, the mounting fear of losing something you possess, coupled with apprehension of the unknown. Sometimes this fear is rationalized by the assumption that some Bolshevik red terror is the only alternative to the present system; sometimes it finds vent in accusing everyone who thinks differently of being un-British, or un-American, as the case may be. But do not let us underrate the power of this fear. A great deal of it is unconscious or at best half-conscious, and is transformed in consciousness into an exaggerated patriotism; or into an emphasis on the value of order and discipline above all else; or into apparently rational arguments proving that any alternative system is bound to lead to economic disaster; or into unreasoning faith in a leader (of which a recent example from a democratic country was the refusal of millions of English men and women to allow a breath of criticism of Mr. Chamberlain).

But it is exceedingly powerful. And it is not solely the economic fear of losing property; there is also the social fear of losing privilege and position, and for many in the so-called upper classes in Britain this is just as potent as economic fear. They are afraid of losing their privilege of ordering others about, of receiving deference from the so-called lower classes, of being 'ladies and gentlemen' instead of merely human beings like everybody else.

What is more, this half-conscious fear that refuses to admit what it is really afraid of, provides a reservoir of power ready to be exploited by the minority who are quite clear in their minds about what they are likely to lose through a democratic transformation of the social system, and are frankly determined to resist it by every means at their disposal. By and large, the leaders of big business in Germany deliberately threw in their lot with the Nazis and shared in exploiting the hazy and undirected fears of the masses. Some of them later discovered their mistake; but that will not deter a great many rich and powerful people in democratic countries from deliberately supporting undemocratic proposals from fear of losing their power or their riches.

Let us make no mistake. Almost without exception, everyone who has anything to lose is afraid of losing it. The rich man is afraid of losing his money, the privileged man his privileges; the petty bourgeois is afraid of losing social caste, the boss of losing his power, the workman of losing his job. To be afraid of losing what you have is natural and inevitable. What we all have to guard against is letting this natural fear weigh too heavily in the scales against the need for change. Our absence of private loss may mean public loss for the community; our temporary gain may later be swallowed up in much more wholesale loss. The essential thing for all who believe in democracy is to cling to that faith and test every system and every new proposal against it. If their belief is genuine, they will reject any measures that diminish democracy, that set up the State above the individual, that subordinate the rights of the many to the interests of the few. And in so doing they will be guarding their country against counter-revolution or the all-too-easy downward path of disguised Fascism.

The lesson of history is plain enough—that threatened systems react blindly and violently, that doomed interests find a desperate vigour and can inflict terrible damage in their last struggles. That is why I have spent so much time on this question of anti-democratic counter-revolution, whether violent or gradual, because it is a very real danger. But if it be urgent for us to be on our guard against reaction, it is even more urgent that we should try to visualize the new kind of society that we want, and to take practical steps to bring it into being. Reintegration is the only answer to disintegration, and democratic reintegration the only effective way of preventing fascist or anti-democratic reintegration.

The trouble is that it is so hard to visualize what is yet unborn, so difficult to paint any picture of the future which shall be convincing enough and real enough to set over against the present that we know. But it must be attempted.

XII

The New Democratic Society

IN THE previous chapter I spoke of the need of some picture, however incomplete, of the reintegrated democracy which we must attain if we are to be safe against chaos on the one hand and some form of Fascism on the other; here I shall try my hand at the difficult business of sketching in the outlines of such a picture.

I have already mentioned Peter Drucker's book, *The End of Economic Man*, in which, with ruthless brilliance, he showed how the ideals of nineteenth-century economic democracy, and of the whole *laisser-faire* capitalist system, were finally collapsing, but without taking the further step of outlining the new system that is destined to replace the old. If what I have said earlier is valid, we shall have to call this new phase of society, the Age of Social Man: instead of an economic individualist society, we shall have an organic society. The Germans have entered on this new phase, but in a totalitarian and militarist form: we must achieve the transition within the frame of democracy.

One way of visualizing the type of society we want is to contrast it with what we don't want—the decaying 'Old Order,' democratic but non-social, of *laisser-faire*, and the emergent 'New Order,' social but anti-democratic, of Nazi Germany. In the organic society of social man, social incentives, group activities, and human interrelations will be the keynotes, and individualist and economic motives will take a secondary place. But in a democratic organic society, the enrichment of the human individual will be the primary aim. Thus we reject the false totalitarian myth by which the State is enthroned as something of higher value than the individual. Equally we reject the authoritarian leadership principle underlying the Nazi system, according to which all authority is delegated downwards, from an irresponsible but all-powerful dictator, through a rigid hierarchy of subordinate leaders, to the masses; we must, on the contrary, build upwards from the individual citizen, with leaders acting through the delegated authority of those whom they represent. We must repudiate the artificial unity created in the totalitarian states, the notion that opinion and truth are matters of dogma and authority. Freedom of speech, of opinion, of discussion, of belief, of research, are vital to a democratic society.

On the other hand, we repudiate certain elements in the democracy of the age of economic man. We deny that the profit motive should be the primary incentive in society; we look to social incentives such as service and self-development. We deny that *laisser-faire* competition is the best method for achieving progress; we recognize the need for collective planning. We deny that the interests of property should be allowed to predominate over social interests: we prefer to think primarily in terms of people. In Britain the 'Old Order' has its own particular characteristics. The liberal principle of economic individualism has been active side by side with the conservative principle of class privilege based on property and on social position. This peculiar combination has its advantages and its disadvantages. It provides us in Britain with a better chance of achieving our transformation peacefully, without any revolutionary bloodshed: but it also makes it easier for this peaceful transformation to go in the direction of disguised Fascism instead of in the direction of a more organic democracy.

This mixture of principles, again, has resulted in the British attitude towards the social services, to which I referred in earlier chapters. Under our conservative class system, the more fortunate tend to think of their duties in terms of alms-giving and *noblesse oblige*, rather than of responsibility in service: to *laisser-faire* liberal tradition, the economic system is a self-regulating and self-improving machine—which unfortunately has developed a few defects. The social services thus came to be thought of as a mixture of charity and of palliatives designed to keep the existing system working.

Meanwhile, however, the powerful monopolies of

western capitalism in its latest phase, from being merely non-social, may easily become anti-social. The converse of this unification of business into larger and more powerful units has been the tendency to de-socialize the individual, who becomes more and more of a social atom, bandied about by impersonal and non-social economic forces. In an organic democracy, every individual, every group and every sectional interest will be tied into the whole by having to assume a set of responsibilities as well as receiving a series of rights.

That will serve as a preliminary approach. But for any sort of concrete picture, we must go further into detail. The social services are, we have already seen, bound to become more unified, and more positive, with the Government playing a more active role; economic planning is bound to continue on an increasing scale, adapting to peacetime needs the various controls introduced during the war. These two trends, taken together, must be directed in the first instance to ensuring security for the individual and stability for the economic system, for security and stability are necessary as the foundations on which more adventurous and, in a sense, more essential, possibilities may be built.

But the biggest change that must be carried through before we can say we have achieved the age of social man—and whether it will take five or fifty years, none can say—is the dethronement of the motives of profit and individual advancement in favour of social motives and social incentives of various kinds. Please do not think I am suggesting that the profit motive will not continue at all, or that people will not go on being ambitious. I am merely saying that these motives will have to take second place instead of first place. We are so used to thinking primarily in terms of the battle for profit and advancement that we find it difficult to conceive of another kind of world. But let us remember that if real economic security is assured through State social services, the world will look very different to many struggling wage-earners. Then, as planning increases in scale and in efficiency, it will remove much of the instability and risk which now besets business enterprise. And a lessening of risk means a lowering of the rate of return on investment. How in detail commercial and industrial concerns will be run is too big a subject to touch on here. We may anticipate that more yields will be compulsorily limited, as, for instance, on the London Passenger Transport Board shares (but to a lower level); possibly the Archbishop of York's suggestion will be adopted, that returns on capital should never run for more than a limited period. Taxation also can play its part. The responsibility of a firm to its workers can be partly embodied in laws about working conditions—ventilation, lighting, space, safety devices, and so on; and perhaps in the partial taking over by industry of the business of looking after the health and recreation of employees.

Then industry will clearly have to take responsibilities in regard to the nation; in the past, industrial policy has often been nationally quite irresponsible, as shown by the selling of war material to potential enemies. Finally, there are the local responsibilities of industry and commerce. These will be enforced under planning legislation of various sorts, making it impossible for the air to be polluted with smoke or the water with poisonous waste—a big public loss for the sake of a little extra private gain—or for a business to destroy amenities or upset a careful plan by dumping down a factory wherever it chooses.

We can, I think, look forward to the time when the people who run most businesses will approximate more and more closely to salaried officials, carrying on their vital job in the joint interests of the community in which they live, their workpeople, and their shareholders. And this will mean the relegation of the profit motive to second place. In some cases it may be in the national interest not to bother about making a profit at all. We have in this country already adopted that principle by giving subsidies to certain kinds of housing and certain types of agriculture which we think ought to get done, profit or no profit. Usually, however, it will still mean that a profit should be shown, but that the job of making that profit as large as possible, irrespective of other considerations, will no longer be allowed to be the dominant feature of business and industry.

But even if, partly by legislation, partly by an increase in salaried officials, partly by a change of attitude, the profit motive does have to take a back seat, we still have to ask what incentives are to be put in its place to make the wheels of society go round.

Here the picture inevitably becomes somewhat misty. But the experience of other ages and other countries, coupled with what has been happening here during the war, at least enables us to see the main types of incentive. Perhaps we can sum them up as the motive of service and sacrifice, the motive of self-development and enjoyment, and the motive of individual and shared creativeness.

I had something to say in a previous section on service in war-time. But how can we continue to canalize the spirit of service into useful channels in peace-time? One needs, it seems to me, a very varied and flexible form of national service. Military service will doubtless continue. It is already varied enough, with its airmen and its technicians, its Pioneer Corps, its armoured divisions, its parachute troops, its seamen. And, as we know from the experience of countries like Switzerland, peace-time military service can be truly democratic.

But we must, I think, look to other forms of service as much as service in the armed forces. Why should not young people be given the opportunity of learning about other kinds of life than the one in which they are going to earn their livelihood later, while at the same time feeling of use to the community? Both boys and girls could serve on the land or on various kinds of public works; boys could elect to go to sea or into an engineering shop; girls could help in hospitals or join a domestic service corps. And for the picked élite, there would be other outlets of various kinds, from youth leadership to research assistance.

This primary form of service-training would presumably last for a year, possibly two years. For adults, there would be short periods of service at yearly or two-yearly intervals. For them, too, many of the same types of service would also be available as outlets. But in addition, there will be many cases where special talent or skill will be called upon for various community projects, from contributing to some new public building to helping in a dramatic or musical organization. And finally one may suggest that at longer intervals, say every five years, the service demanded of adult men and women will be attendance at a course of instruction which will serve partly as a refresher course in their own particular job, partly as a means of keeping their minds fresh and bright in relation to the world's general problems.

Here, service becomes linked up with self-development. This is an equally important incentive, and in many ways complementary to service. People want to lose themselves in a greater whole, to sacrifice themselves for something larger than themselves; but they also want to make the most out of their individual selves, by all methods from arduous self-development, through self-expression, to light-hearted enjoyment. And both motives must be given scope.

What sort of outlets should social man be given for his self-development and his enjoyment? Here I must content myself with throwing out a few tentative ideas. First of all, it seems both necessary and desirable that the community should take a hand in culture and recreation—or if you prefer it, that culture and recreation should become a part of the social services. We have got so used to thinking of social services from the negative and palliative point of view, as rather drab organizations concerned with the relief of unemployment or ill-health or old age. But once they are conceived in a positive spirit, there is every reason for including in them constructive schemes for dealing with the highest and most cheerful activities of men.

At present recreation has become very much commercialized. The result is increasing standardization of amusement, destined for consumption by increasingly passive spectators. We need organizations which will help us to become active participants, whether in sport or the enjoyment of wild nature, in music, in the drama, in travel. Voluntary effort is no longer sufficient to ensure this; we need active organizations, on the municipal, the regional, and the national level.

We also need planning to give us the physical organs of culture and recreation. At the moment we are, as Priestley has put it, a predominantly urban civilization with precious little urban culture. Our towns and cities, under the chaos of profit-seeking *laisser-faire*, have become so many mechanisms for frustrating numerous aspects of life. But a city, if properly designed, can be a mechanism for intensifying certain sides of life to a pitch that is not possible elsewhere. Through its architecture and its parks, it can create physical beauty; through concert-halls and cinemas and picture galleries and theatres it can provide art; through stadia and recreation grounds it can give opportunities to the body; through meeting-rooms and libraries, churches and public squares it can afford outlets for social meetings, political discussions, adult education, and mass ceremonial.

Only if culture and recreation become truly a social service, and the opportunities for them are planned on a large scale, can society become truly self-conscious. The Greek city states and the Italian cities of the late Middle Ages and early Renaissance were such communities, but only a section of the people shared in their self-conscious community culture and the fullness of their life: today, through universal education and through advances in technology, such as printing, the films and wireless, all might participate.

During the early years of the New Deal, a beginning was made in these directions. The artists' and writers' and theatre projects under the W.P.A. did lay the foundations of a community culture for the United States. Unfortunately, they were conceived in terms of relief for an emergency, and have now been discontinued.

We in Britain have been without community culture for so long that we are suspicious of it. Culture sounds highbrow, and is looked upon as something apart, for the peculiar few. It happens, however, to be a fact that art can provide both new understanding of life for individuals, and also unique ways of expressing the life of the community. In the recent past, art has been almost wholly divorced from its social function; and most good artists have become mere individuals, often frustrated individuals, instead of the agents by which society as a whole, and the common man in society, can realize possibilities that would otherwise remain latent. In the age of social man, art and beauty must be made to play their due part, as well as simple recreation and enjoyment.

In art, the motive of self-development and expression is linked up with that of creativeness. But creativeness can be given many other outlets. In so far as the gigantic social experiment of the U.S.S.R. has been successful, it owes its success largely to the feeling among the common people that they, by their own work, are helping to create something of value for themselves. This incentive, of shared creativeness, has been largely lacking in our *laisser-faire* democracies. The more it can be encouraged, the more rapid our progress is likely to be towards a truly organic society. Perhaps we ought, like Nazi Germany, to borrow a leaf from the Russian's book, and proclaim a concrete plan for Britain, to be realized in so many years. This would put the incentives of service and of creativeness in double harness, with the spur of a definite goal to keep them from flagging.

Much of what I have been saying will, I am sure, have sounded extremely Utopian. How, for instance, can you put young men on trawlers or in engineering works to do their national service—will not that throw regular workers out of a job? Trades Unions would never stand for that sort of thing. . . . The answer is that if the new system is really efficient in reducing unemployment, in increasing security, and in giving a decent life to the few who are temporarily out of work, this question will not arise. In fact, as in Nazi Germany, we may find ourselves in a condition of under-employment if we can once mobilize all our resources for social ends; seen from the social angle, a great many problems will look very different from what they do today. But here we are back again at the basic difficulty of drawing any convincing picture of a state of affairs which doesn't yet exist. All I can do, in conclusion, is to say that I believe it *can* be made to exist, and that a transformed democracy of some such sort as this is the only real hope for the world. It will not bring any millennium. Inevitably, after the war, we shall have to face a long period of hard work and low standards of living. But it will harness new forces of human nature, which have not been given due scope during the *laisser-faire* age of economic man; it will harness them on a mass scale, and in the service of hope.

DATE DUE